MW00856978

Paul's Three Paths to Salvation

Paul's Three Paths to Salvation

Gabriele Boccaccini

William B. Eerdmans Publishing Company
Grand Rapids, Michigan

Wm. B. Eerdmans Publishing Co.
4035 Park East Court SE, Grand Rapids, Michigan 49546
www.eerdmans.com

© 2020 Gabriele Boccaccini
All rights reserved
Published 2020
Printed in the United States of America

26 25 24 23 22 21 20 1 2 3 4 5 6 7

ISBN 978-0-8028-3921-3

Library of Congress Cataloging-in-Publication Data

Names: Boccaccini, Gabriele, 1958– author.
Title: Paul's three paths to salvation / Gabriele Boccaccini.
Description: Grand Rapids, Michigan : William B. Eerdmans Publishing Company, 2020. | Includes bibliographical references and index. | Summary: "A historical argument that Paul's teachings suggest three different methods of salvation"—Provided by publisher.
Identifiers: LCCN 2020013214 | ISBN 9780802839213 (hardcover)
Subjects: LCSH: Bible. Epistles of Paul--Theology. | Salvation—Biblical teaching.
Classification: LCC BS2655.S25 B63 2020 | DDC 234—dc23
LC record available at https://lccn.loc.gov/2020013214

Unless otherwise indicated, all Scripture quotations are from New Revised Standard Version Bible, copyright © 1989 National Council of the Churches of Christ in the United States of America. Used by permission. All rights reserved worldwide.

For Aloma

CONTENTS

FOREWORD

It hardly needs to be said that no figure in Christian history, with the exception of Jesus himself, has been of greater consequence for the tradition than Paul. The whole of Christian dogmatic and "systematic" theology either grows directly out of his epistles or is inflected through them. And yet no other figure in Christian history has suffered greater or more grievous misrepresentations by his putative followers. In part, this is attributable to an undeniable and fairly frequent obscurity in Paul's way of expressing himself; he was, as even his most devoted readers should be willing to admit, a careless writer. His style was almost invariably precipitate, fragmentary, syntactically vagrant—even sprawling. This is not to deny that there is also a very real eloquence in his prose, at times almost exquisite; but it is an eloquence born from passion rather than from literary refinement or dialectical precision. As often as not, the reader is not so much led on by the clarity and rigor of his arguments as carried along by the visionary intensity of his voice. That said, the far greater cause of the misunderstandings that have bedeviled Paul's posterity has been a loss of context—cultural, religious, linguistic, and philosophical. Paul lived and wrote as a faithful Jew in a first-century world, within the context of a Judaism that was both Semitic and Graeco-Roman, that had absorbed influences from the Persian and Greek intellectual worlds, and that had not yet fully evolved the rabbinic traditions of later centuries. He thought in categories at once eminently Jewish and pervasively Hellenistic, but also apocalyptic, messianic, metaphysical, and prophetic; and the Second Temple Judaism in which he had been reared was far more religiously diverse and intellectually heterogeneous than most of us today are likely to appreciate. But, by the time Augustine's fully elaborated "Pauline synthesis" of Christian thought took shape, Paul's readers were living in a Christian context, one in which much of the intellectual and spiritual world that Paul had known had vanished, and in which even the schools of Judaism that were still active were little understood.

This was especially true in the Christian West, where—in addition to all the other obstacles that made a proper reading of Paul difficult—there was the barrier of language. Augustine, for instance—the greatest of the Latin fathers, among the greatest minds of Christian history, and one of the first truly "systematic" interpreters of Paul in theological history—was separated from Paul's world not only by his ignorance of apocalyptic Judaism in the first century, or of the angelology and demonology of the Second Temple "Noachian" books, or of countless other things that were essential to the apostle's vision of reality, but also by an inability to read Greek. In the end, for all his genius, Augustine more or less invented a Paul who never truly existed and then bequeathed him to later generations of Western believers. In the works of his late period in particular, Augustine (guilelessly but nonetheless disastrously) took Paul's claim that it is not ritual observances like circumcision and kosher dietary laws that place humans in a "just" or "righteous" relation to God and converted it into the very different claim that human beings are wholly impotent to please God through "works" or "deeds" of any kind (including works of moral righteousness). He also made Paul's authentic description of humanity as a family born in slavery to sin and death more or less interchangeable with an entirely spurious discourse regarding humanity's inherited culpability as a single *massa damnata*. Moreover, whether or not he was the first theologian illegitimately to conflate the ideas of "justification" and "salvation" in Paul's thought, he was certainly the most influential to do so. And he, more than any other theologian in Christian history, was responsible for turning Paul's quite explicit teaching that human beings will be judged by God according to their works into an elliptical and willfully opaque teaching that, on the day of judgment, God will merely crown his own merits in those souls to which he has imparted them by the sheer grace of unmerited election.

This is the Paul who dominated Western Christian thought throughout most of its centuries, whether gladly accepted or partially resisted by ecclesiastical authority and theologians. It is the Paul of Prosper of Aquitaine and Fulgentius Ruspensis, as well as of (in a more controversial and extreme expression) Gottschalk; it is also the Paul of the early modern period—of Luther, and Calvin and Jansen, as well as of the baroque Thomists. And it is the Paul, also—most tragically of all—of certain persistent Christian denigrations and caricatures of Judaism. Whereas the Paul of the epistles was a Jew who saw the gospel as taking away the wall of division between the true children of the covenant and gentiles, so that all might receive God's forgiveness and live in righteousness, this mythological Paul was a Christian who had rejected the "legalism" and "works righteousness" of Judaism. Even those modern, "revisionist" readings of Paul that have so vastly improved on this picture (that of E. P. Sanders perhaps most epochally) have still tended to preserve aspects of some of its more reductive treatments of an "antithesis" between law and gospel. Even many scholars who have striven to locate Paul more firmly in a Jewish cultural context and Jewish theological idiom have tended in the process to invent a Christianized picture of first-century Judaism—a kind of Protestantism without Jesus—concocted from a mixture of the late prophets and much later rabbinic traditions, and purged of Second Temple apocalyptic ideas and of all "foreign" influences (Persian, Hellenistic, and so forth).

And, in a sense, that is very much where today's Western Christian tends to stand. Ask, for instance, the average American Christian—say, some genial Presbyterian who attends church regularly and owns a New International Version of the Bible—what gospel the apostle Paul preached. The reply will usually fall along predictable lines: Human beings, bearing the guilt of original sin and destined for eternal hell, cannot save themselves through good deeds, or make themselves acceptable to God; yet God, in his mercy, sent the eternal Son to offer himself up for our sins, and now the righteousness of Christ has been graciously imputed or imparted to all who have faith; though, even then, this company of the faithful comprises only those whom God, in his inscrutable counsels and without any regard to prevision of their merits or demerits, sovereignly elects for the gratuitous gift of salvation, while consigning the rest of humanity to a condign eternal torment. Some details might vary, but not the basic story. And, admittedly, some of the tale's language is reminiscent of terms used by Paul, at least as filtered through certain conventional translations; but much of it is a fantasy. For one thing, it presumes elements of later Christian belief that are absent from Paul's own writings. Some of these (like the idea that humans are born damnably guilty in God's eyes, or the notion that good deeds are not required for salvation) arise from a history of misleading translations. Others (like the concept of an eternal hell of conscious torment) are entirely imagined, attributed to Paul on the basis of some mistaken picture of what the New Testament as a whole teaches. And, on the whole, I think it fair to say, a certain long history of misreadings of the Letter to the Romans—and especially chapters 9–11—has created an impression of his theological concerns so entirely alien to the conceptual world the real Paul inhabited that he now occupies scarcely any place at all in Christian memory.

I find much to admire in Gabriele Boccaccini's attempt to reconstruct Paul's own vision of salvation in this book. Perhaps its most important contribution is the rescue it effects of Paul's language of righteousness and grace from the received readings of the magisterial Reformation. It is true, obviously, that Paul does address the issue of "righteousness" or "justice," and asserts that this is something available to us only through a virtue he calls πίστις (*pistis*)—"faith" or "trust" or even "fidelity." But that virtue is explicitly one that largely consists in or inevitably entails works of obedience to God and love of others, and the only ἔργα (*erga*), "works," that Paul claims make no necessary contribution to personal sanctity in God's eyes are the purely ritual observances prescribed by the law of Moses. Moreover, the chief importance of this for Paul is simply that the separation between Jews and gentiles has been annulled in Christ, opening salvation equally to all peoples, whether they are capable of the law or not. In the end, though, once the true terms of "righteousness" are established for Jew and gentile alike, all are still called to stand before the throne of God's justice, to be judged according to things they have done or have failed to do.

For myself, though, I have to admit that what I find most admirable about Boccaccini's book is its emphasis upon Paul's larger narrative of salvation: the epic, that is, of Christ's defeat of the malign spiritual agencies that rule the fallen cosmos. At least, if I were asked to summarize Paul's actual teachings, relying only on the authentic epistles (along with the *dubia* of Ephesians and Colossians), I think I would tend to identify his principal point of emphasis not as sin and righteousness but as the overthrow of bad angels. I believe, at any rate, that Boccaccini is right to start here, and to accord this theme the attention it has so often been denied in theological scholarship. To my mind, the essence of Paul's theology is something far stranger, and is played out on an immeasurably vaster scale, than most Christians would find it comfortable to contemplate. For him, we are living in the final days of one world-age that is rapidly passing, and are awaiting the dawn of another that will differ from it radically in every dimension: heavenly and terrestrial, spiritual and physical. In the story of salvation, nothing less than the entire cosmos is at stake, and the great drama at the heart of that story is one of invasion, conquest, spoliation, and triumph. For Paul, creation has been made subject to Death, to whom we have been enslaved by our sin and by the ill governance of "angelic" or "daemonian" agencies, both reigning over the earth from the heavens above and holding spirits in thrall below the earth. These agencies—these Archons, these angelic beings and elemental spirits whom Paul calls Thrones and Powers and Dominations and Spiritual Forces of Evil in the High Places—are the gods of the nations who are not "gods by nature." Perhaps even the angels who watch over Israel (so the Letter to the Galatians hints) are of their number. These spiritual powers may be wholly fallen, or at least mutinous, or merely deficient caretakers of the world; they are certainly deficient legislators in the deliverance of the law; but, whatever the case, they stand intractably between us and God. Yet Christ, in descending to Hades and ascending again through the heavens, has vanquished all the Powers below and above that separate us from the love of God. All that remains to happen is the consummation of the present cosmic age: Christ will appear again, now in his full glory as universal conqueror, having subordinated all the cosmic Powers to himself—literally, having properly "ordered" them "under" himself—and then, at the last, will hand over the whole of this reclaimed empire to the Father. Then the cosmos will be ruled no longer through wicked or incompetent spiritual intermediaries, but directly by God. The new age that is coming, moreover—when creation will be transformed into the kingdom of God and the frame of nature charged with divine glory—will be an age of "spirit" rather than "flesh," in which the "psychical body"—the "ensouled" or "animal" way of life—will be replaced by a "spiritual body," beyond the reach of death.

I should not, however, dilate so freely on the matter. This is not my book. Suffice it to say that Boccaccini's treatment of the sources and significance of Paul's angelology and demonology, and indeed of his whole cosmic vision, is exemplary, and I do not wish to trespass upon it here. The same is true of his treatment of Paul's messianism. But there too I should not overstay my welcome.

I will add only one observation, in the hope that Boccaccini might address it—or at least the concerns informing it—in further detail at some future date. He is, of course, quite correct to argue that, for Paul, that act of forgiveness by which God places both Jews and gentiles in a "justified" condition is not yet the final verdict on any soul, and that Paul believes all will still ultimately be judged according to their works. But there is also something of a notorious ambiguity in Paul's language on just this matter of eschatological vindication and condemnation. He never, of course, speaks of some eternal hell of torment for unregenerate souls. Rather, at least in many of the places where he addresses the final fate of the wicked, he seems to suggest that the derelict will perish along with the age that is passing. At other times, however, and no less frequently, he speaks as if ultimately all human beings will be saved (Rom 5:18, for instance, or 1 Cor 15:22). And, of course, this same ambiguity runs throughout the New Testament as a whole. It is not obvious that Paul ever settled on one exact understanding of the eventual state of a redeemed creation or of a redeemed humanity *in toto*. It is hard not to wonder whether the "anyone" of 1 Corinthians 3:14–15 should be taken literally, with precisely as expansive a range of reference as the pronoun would seem to suggest. And this raises at least one question regarding the workings of grace for Paul that Boccaccini might address at greater length. For, while it is true that Paul insists that we shall be judged according to our works, there seems here to be a suggestion that there is yet a further dimension of that initial grace of justification, one that far exceeds simply the "new beginning" it grants to Jews and gentiles in this world. Even in that final act of discrimination, these verses seem to say, that same grace may transform even condemnation into redemption, so that ultimately mercy triumphs over judgment (to quote an author, one whose own view of "Pauline" theology is a matter of some dispute). Whatever one thinks of the "universalist" pericopes in Paul's writings, this does seem somewhat to complicate our understanding of what differentiates justification from salvation, as well as of what unites them.

As I say, though, a question for another time. This is a splendid and necessary book, and it is an honor to have been chosen not only to be present at its launch but also to enjoy the privilege of smashing the champagne bottle against its bow.

David Bentley Hart

PREFACE

Paul was not a prophet of doom for unbelievers but the herald of a merciful God who wants everyone to be saved. The apostle accomplished his task by proclaiming God's justice to the righteous (Jews and gentiles alike) and God's forgiveness to repentant sinners (Jews and gentiles alike) in the imminence of the last judgment.

There may be irony in presenting Paul as a Second Temple Jew and a messenger of God's mercy. Wasn't he the destroyer of Judaism, the creator of Christianity as a separate religion, the herald of a "new" religion of grace that replaced the "old" religion of works? And wasn't he the one who condemned to hell all who do not admit to being sinners and do not believe in Jesus Christ as their Savior?

As a specialist of Second Temple Judaism, I have never been satisfied with this approach, which made Paul the greatest theologian of the new faith, but also the apostate of Judaism and the father of intolerance against the unbelievers. Yet almost irresistibly his figure attracted and fascinated me. The more he was presented as the one who superseded Judaism, the more he appeared to me as a Jew of his own time, perfectly at ease in that Jewish environment which he supposedly considered a cage from which Christianity was to be freed. The more his teaching was taken as justification for hatred and intolerance, the more he appeared to me as a model of inclusion and universal salvation.

Since the 1980s, Paul has always been in my view a Jewish apocalyptic author, much more acquainted with the tradition of Enoch than with Greek philosophy, much closer to the Synoptics and Acts than to the Gospel of John. Paul's problems (origin of evil, forgiveness of sins, salvation, inclusion of gentiles) were the problems of his age; even his more "original" answers were compatible with the diversity of Second Temple Judaism, no more daring and controversial than other answers provided by other contemporaneous Jewish authors.

Paul has become a recurring theme in my graduate and undergraduate courses. He was the focus of two international conferences I organized in Rome in 2014 and 2016. More recently, I was invited as a speaker to Pauline conferences in Amsterdam and Bratislava, as well as to the Meeting of the International Council of Christians and Jews in Rome. A panel discussion with Mark Nanos at the 2018 SBL Meeting in Denver gave me the opportunity to share my ideas with some of those scholars who today are most committed to recovering Paul's Jewishness and his role in Second Temple Judaism.

At the 2014 conference in Rome I presented a paper, then published in the proceedings I edited with Carlos A. Segovia, in which for the first time I offered a synthesis of my vision of Paul: "The Three Paths to Salvation of Paul the Jew," in Gabriele Boccaccini and Carlos A. Segovia, eds., *Paul the Jew: Rereading the Apostle as a Figure of Second Temple Judaism* (Minneapolis: Fortress, 2016), 1–19. The breaking point of my research was when I began to realize that Paul's message of justification by faith was not addressed indiscriminately to all (Jews and gentiles alike), nor exclusively to gentiles but specifically to the many—the sinners (Jews and gentiles alike). The Book of the Parables of Enoch appeared to me as the key text for understanding the message of Jesus and Paul, with its emphasis on the possibility of forgiveness offered to repentant sinners at the end of time.

Once I recovered the apocalyptic context of Paul's preaching and his intended audience, everything suddenly looked clear. Paul was no longer alone in total uniqueness but was in continuity with the apocalyptic discourse that began with the Enochic tradition and was carried on by the Synoptic tradition. By "justification by faith" he did not mean salvation by faith in the last judgment but forgiveness by faith in the imminence of the last judgment, which will remain according to each one's deeds. Paul was not a prophet of doom but a messenger of God's mercy for sinners.

Now that the walls that for centuries have divided Jewish studies from New Testament studies, the canonical from the noncanonical, and the Jewish from the Christian have finally begun to crumble, we can celebrate Paul's return to the house he never abandoned, not as a prodigal son but as a legitimate member of the family. And we can do it without downplaying the role he played in establishing that Jewish messianic and apocalyptic group that would later develop into what we now call Christianity. We no longer need to separate Paul from Judaism to claim his Christianness, nor do we need to separate him from Christianity in order to affirm his Jewishness. Paul was a Second Temple Jew and a leader of the early Jesus movement.

There are too many friends and colleagues I should name and thank for the inspiration they gave me for the composition of this volume. Since 2001 the Enoch Seminar has put me in conversation with many of the most distinguished specialists in Second Temple Judaism and Christian origins. With the exception of my teacher at the University of Turin, Paolo Sacchi, and the two vice-directors of the Enoch Seminar, Kelley Coblentz Bautch and Loren Stuckenbruck, I will not even try to make a list of my closest friends. They know how much I appreciate their friendship and how much I owe them for their scholarship. Many of them recently surprised me by contributing to my Festschrift for my 60th birthday: *Wisdom Poured Out Like Water: Studies on Jewish and Christian Antiquity in Honor of Gabriele Boccaccini*, ed. J. Harold Ellens, et al. (Berlin: de Gruyter, 2018). I am truly grateful for this.

Here I would like to remember those who have passed away but whose presence and teaching are still vivid with gratitude in my memory: Hanan Eshel, Francesco Adorno, Jan Alberto Soggin, Alan F. Segal, Carlo Maria Martini, Clara Kraus Reggiani, Jacob Neusner, Louis Feldman, Giovanni Garbini, Philip R. Davies, J. Harold Ellens, Lea Sestieri, Klaus Koch, Geza Xeravitz, and Larry Hurtado. Together with my parents Walter and Maria Adelaide, my in-laws Dino and Manola, my grandparents Ada, Camillo and Elena, my great aunts Gina and Linda, my uncles and aunts Valerio and

Marisa, Wilma and Ezio, and my cousin Filippo, they have a special place in my heart where I can always visit them. They will continue to be with me as long as I live. A particular group of friends, however, I cannot help mentioning. Since the early 1990s, my experience at Michigan has been blessed with meeting talented students, such as J. Harold Ellens, Philip Munoa, April DeConick, Charles Gieschen, Mark Kinzer, Lynne Alcott Kogel, Ronald Ruark, Jason von Ehrenkrook, James Waddell, Isaac Oliver, Jason Zurawski, Deborah Forger, Rodney Caruthers, and Joshua Scott. Together we shared unforgettable moments of learning and created a community of ideas that has not been interrupted by being now scattered all around the globe. I am very grateful to each of them, and particularly to Isaac Oliver for his insightful remarks, and to Ronald Ruark, with whom I had the opportunity to discuss the topics presented in this volume.

I could not have achieved anything without the constant love and support of my wife, Aloma Bardi, to whom this book is dedicated. We happily spent 40 years together and shared the joy of marriage and scholarly research. With even greater expectations and happiness, we look forward to the years ahead.

Gabriele Boccaccini

Chapter 1

Paul the Jew and Paul the Christian

Paul the Hatred Hater

In an age of resurgent religious intolerance, Jews, Christians, and Muslims are challenged to prove that monotheistic religions are not intrinsically intolerant and exclusive but are indeed capable of inspiring and uniting people of goodwill in peace and coexistence. Centuries of conflicts demonstrate that this has not always been the case. Made aware of the problem by their own experience as victims and perpetrators of violence, the children of Abraham are compelled to examine themselves and face their own evil and the roots of hatred and intolerance lurking in their own religious traditions and beliefs.[1]

It is only a matter of intellectual honesty to admit that on the road to interfaith dialogue and mutual respect, Paul of Tarsus looks more like an obstacle than a facilitator. Born a Jew, he became a Christian, making manifest with his own conversion and teaching that all unbelievers (or believers in other religions) are doomed unless they also convert and submit themselves to the Christian messiah in the same way he did. Among those condemned by their guilty unbelief are his fellow Jews, once the chosen people of God but now deprived of all dignity, since the new covenant in Christ superseded and made obsolete the old covenant with Moses. At least, this is what we are commonly told.

1. J. Harold Ellens, ed., *The Destructive Power of Religion: Violence in Judaism, Christianity, and Islam*, 4 vols. (Santa Barbara, CA: Praeger, 2004).

To be sure, Paul in his letters never spoke the language of hatred, nor "followed the modern fundamentalist tactic of first convincing people that they were sinners and in need of salvation."[2] At the center of Paul's preaching was a message of inclusiveness and salvation—the good news of the grace of God revealed in Christ, the "message of reconciliation" given to the world (2 Cor 5:19). Acknowledging Paul's goodwill, however, doesn't exonerate him from the hateful consequences of his message or from building an impenetrable wall of intolerance between believers and unbelievers. Everybody (Jew and gentile, male and female, free and slave) is called and welcomed, but there is only one path to salvation in Christ for converts.

Should we then accept the paradox of a message of grace that generated hatred and a message of inclusion that generated exclusion? Or should we deny Paul and expose him as a champion of intolerance—the "genius of hatred," as Friedrich Nietzsche denounced him,[3] or to put it in more colorful contemporaneous vocabulary, "a racist, chauvinist jerk"?[4] Should we hate the hater? Or should we just forget Paul and choose a more tolerant path *in spite of* him? Or should we pursue with renewed commitment the task of recovering his authentic message, test it with the fire of modern criticism, and see if it can be redeemed from a long tradition of intolerance?

Paul against Judaism

In the context of first-century Judaism, Paul's figure appears to be among the most enigmatic and difficult to grasp. A halo of mystery, if not the curse

2. E. P. Sanders, *Paul and Palestinian Judaism: A Comparison of Patterns of Religion* (London: SCM, 1977), 444.

3. In the words of Nietzsche, Paul "is the genius of hatred, in the standpoint of hatred, and in the relentless logic of hatred." See John J. Gager, *Reinventing Paul* (Oxford: Oxford University Press, 2000), 9; and Jörg Salaquarda, "Dionysius versus the Crucified One: Nietzsche's Understanding of the Apostle Paul," in *Studies in Nietzsche and the Judaeo-Christian Tradition*, ed. James C. O'Flaherty, et al. (Chapel Hill: University of North Carolina Press, 1985), 100–29.

4. E. Randolph Richards, *Paul Behaving Badly: Was the Apostle a Racist, Chauvinist Jerk?* (Downers Grove, IL: InterVarsity Press, 2016); Karen Armstrong, *St. Paul: The Apostle We Love to Hate* (Boston: New Harvest, Houghton Mifflin Harcourt, 2015).

of an ancient taboo, still hovers around him, making a firm understanding of his experience difficult. Already in 2 Peter we are warned that in the letters of Paul "there are some things in them hard to understand, which the ignorant and unstable twist to their own destruction" (2 Pet 3:16). In hindsight it looks more like a prophecy than a warning.

On Paul weighs not only the cumbersome reputation of being the first great systematic theologian of nascent Christianity, but also the suspicion—if not the accusation—of having laid the foundations of a poisonous polemic against the torah and the people of Israel, a harbinger of prejudice, intolerance, and discrimination, up to the tragedy of the Holocaust.

It can't be easily overlooked that for centuries Paul has been praised by Christians, and blamed by Jews, for separating Christianity from Judaism. "None has produced more animosity between Jews and Christians. . . . Paul has long been regarded as the source for Christian hatred of Jews and Judaism. . . . [He] turned his back on his former life as a Jew and became the spokesman for early Christian anti-Judaism."[5] Paul appeared to Christians as a theological giant, the convert who unmasked and denounced the futility and weakness (if not the wickedness) of Judaism, but to Jews as a traitor who made a mockery of the faith of his ancestors and became the father of Christian anti-Semitism.[6]

According to the traditional view, Judaism, the (bad) religion of works, was the antithesis of Christianity, the (good) religion of grace. Many aspects of Paul's thought might be rooted in Judaism, but ultimately Paul rejected Judaism because of its many faults.[7]

There were two elements that Paul found especially wrong in Judaism—its legalism and its particularism. For early twentieth-century New Testament scholars, whose knowledge of Judaism was mediated by the works of Ferdinand Wilhelm Weber and Wilhelm Bousset,[8] it could not

5. Gager, *Reinventing Paul*, 3–4.

6. Magnus Zetterholm, *Approaches to Paul: A Student's Guide to Recent Scholarship* (Minneapolis: Fortress, 2009).

7. Henry St. John Thackeray, *The Relation of St. Paul to Contemporary Jewish Thought* (London: Macmillan, 1900).

8. Ferdinand Wilhelm Weber, *System der altsynagogalen palästinischen Theologie aus Targum, Midrasch und Talmud* (Leipzig: Dörffling & Franke, 1880); and Wilhelm

have been otherwise. In order to affirm the grace of Christianity, Paul had to denounce Judaism as a legalistic religion—faith could shine only by rejecting works. And in order to affirm his universalistic project, Paul had to fight against Jewish particularism—his teaching represented a decisive transition from religious particularism to religious universalism.

Early Jewish interpreters were puzzled by the weight of Jewish elements in Paul's thought but nonetheless generally accepted the Christian idea that Paul rejected the torah and abolished the distinction between Jews and gentiles, which from the Jewish point of view made him a renegade and apostate.[9]

The rediscovery of the Jewishness of Jesus, which since the end of the nineteenth century engaged Jewish and Christian scholars in a joint effort, contributed to further digging the furrow. The more the figure of the Master proved to be compatible with the spirit and the practices of Judaism, the more his most famous disciple appeared to be a divisive man, the founder of a religion incompatible with Judaism. "Jesus, yes; Paul, never!" is how Richard Rubenstein in *My Brother Paul* (1972) summarized the Jewish attitude toward Paul.[10] Already in the tenth century, the Karaite leader Yaqub al Qirqisani opposed Jesus to Paul, the unjustly persecuted Jewish teacher to his unfaithful disciple, whom he considered the authentic creator of Christianity.[11] The idea has remained popular in Jewish circles up to the present, still offered as a viable scholarly thesis in the 1980s by Hyam Maccoby.[12]

Bousset, *Die Religion des Judentums im neutestamentlichen Zeitalter* (Berlin: Reuther & Reichard, 1903).

9. Nancy Fuchs-Kreimer, *The "Essential Heresy": Paul's View of the Law according to Jewish Writers, 1886–1986* (PhD diss., Temple University, 1990); Stefan Meissner, *Heimholung des Ketzers. Studies zur jüdischen Auseinandersetzung mit Paulus* (Tübingen: Mohr Siebeck, 1996).

10. Richard L. Rubenstein, *My Brother Paul* (New York: Harper & Row, 1972), 114.

11. Bruno Chiesa and Wilfrid Lockwood, *Ya'qub al-Qirqisani on Jewish Sects and Christianity* (Frankfurt am Main: Peter Lang, 1984).

12. Hyam Maccoby, *The Mythmaker: Paul and the Invention of Christianity* (London: Weidenfeld & Nicolson, 1986).

Early Criticism of the Traditional Paul

Yet there's something not quite right about this view of Paul. Among the leaders of the early Jesus movement, Paul was the one who most strongly claimed his Jewishness against his opponents ("Are they Hebrews? So am I. Are they Israelites? So am I. Are they descendants of Abraham? So am I," 2 Cor 11:22), defended the irrevocability of the divine promises ("Has God rejected his people? By no means!" Rom 11:1), and most readily reiterated the privileges of Israel in the face of the zeal of the new converts among the gentiles ("You, a wild olive shoot . . . do not boast over the branches. . . . Remember that it is not you that support the root, but the root that supports you," Rom 11:17–18).

As a result, the traditional view of Paul has never been without its critics. At the beginning of the twentieth century, Jewish specialists in rabbinic Judaism and New Testament, such as Solomon Schechter and Claude G. Montefiore, repeated in their work that Judaism hardly fits the features of legalism and hatred of the world that Christian scholars like Weber and Bousset identified as its major (and timeless) features.[13] According to Montefiore, Paul might have been right in his criticism of what he knew as Judaism, but he was a Hellenistic Jew who had only a limited and distorted knowledge of mainstream (rabbinic) Judaism.

William Wrede and Albert Schweitzer took a different direction to recover the Jewishness of Paul.[14] They found little continuity between Paul and Hellenism. In their view, Paul was an apocalyptic Jew who "expected his Christ to vanquish the evil powers of the world, including the demons, and

13. Solomon Schechter, *Aspects of Rabbinic Theology* (New York: Macmillan, 1909); Claude G. Montefiore, *Judaism and St. Paul: Two Essays* (London: Max Goschen, 1914).

14. William Wrede, *Paulus* (Halle: Gebauer-Schwetschke, 1904; 2nd ed. [Tübingen: Mohr Siebeck, 1907]; ET: *Paul*, trans. Edward Lummis [London: Philip Green, 1907]); Albert Schweitzer, *Geschichte der Paulinischen Forschung* (Tübingen: Mohr Siebeck, 1911; ET: *Paul and His Interpreters: A Critical History*, trans. William Montgomery [London: Adam and Charles Black, 1912]); and *Die Mystik des Apostels Paulus* (Tübingen: Mohr Siebeck, 1930; ET: *The Mysticism of Paul the Apostle*, trans. William Montgomery [London: Adam and Charles Black, 1931]).

to inaugurate a new condition of things."[15] Montefiore and Schweitzer were outspoken in denouncing the bias (and anti-Semitism) of many of their colleagues, and so were George Foot Moore in 1921 in the United States and James Parkes in 1936 in England.[16] However, any call to change the terms of the conversation remained unanswered. In an era of rampant anti-Semitism, Christian anti-Judaism fed, and was fueled by, popular prejudice against Judaism. Anyone who emphasized Paul's Jewishness, the value of Judaism, and the debt of early Christianity to Second Temple Jewish culture and religion was and remained an isolated voice. Pauline scholars and Second Temple specialists were then on the same page, in perfect agreement in describing Judaism in the age of Jesus as *Spätjudentum* ("late Judaism")—an age of religious decadence after the spiritual heights of biblical prophecy.[17] The Institute for the Study and Eradication of Jewish Influence on German Church Life,[18] directed by Walter Grundmann between 1939 and 1945, may be disregarded today as an aberration of anti-Semitism, but at the time was viewed by many beyond the boundaries of Nazi Germany as a respectable theological enterprise.[19]

The New Perspective on Paul

The war and the Holocaust forced Christians to rethink their relations with the Jews and Judaism. The Jewishness of Jesus immediately became a central point of discussion in the work of Jules Isaac and in the Jewish-Christian agenda defined at Seelisberg.[20] At the same time, the rediscovery

15. Wrede, *Paul*, 153.

16. George F. Moore, "Christian Writers on Judaism," *Harvard Theological Review* 14 (1921): 197–254; James Parkes, *Jesus, Paul, and the Jews* (London: Student Christian Movement Press, 1936).

17. Alfred Bertholet, *Das religionsgeschichtliche Problem des Spätjudentums* (Tübingen: Mohr Siebeck, 1909).

18. *Institut zur Erforschung und Beseitigung des jüdischen Einflusses auf das deutsche kirchliche Leben.*

19. Susannah Heschel, *The Aryan Jesus: Christian Theologians and the Bible in Nazi Germany* (Princeton, NJ: Princeton University Press, 2008).

20. Jules Isaac, *Jésus et Israël* (Paris: Michel, 1948).

of the Dead Sea Scrolls was leading specialists in Second Temple Judaism to a new path—a path of vibrant diversity, very different from the stereotypes of the past.

Pauline scholarship remained initially (and surprisingly) unaffected by these changes. The same old clichés about Jewish legalism and particularism were commonly repeated in the 1950s.

The English translation of Rudolf Bultmann's *Theologie des Altes Testament*, published in 1951, reiterated the same basic contrast between grace and law:

> The contrast between Paul and Judaism consists not merely in his assertion of the present reality of righteousness, but also in a much more decisive thesis—the one which concerns the condition to which God's acquitting decision is tied. The Jew takes it for granted that this condition is keeping the Law, the accomplishing of "works" prescribed by the Law. In direct contrast to this view Paul's thesis runs—to consider its negative aspect first: "*without works of the Law*." . . . The negative aspect of Paul's thesis does not stand alone; a positive statement takes its place beside it: "*by, or from, faith*."[21]

And without any consideration of the recent tragedy of the Holocaust, William Barclay reaffirmed the traditional stereotype that the hatred of the world against the Jews only mirrored their own hatred against the world: "Christianity began with one tremendous problem. Clearly the message of Christianity was meant for all men. . . . But the fact remained that Christianity was cradled in Judaism; and, humanly speaking, no message which was meant for all the world could even have had a more unfortunate cradle. The Jews were involved in a double hatred—the world hated them and they hated the world."[22]

These words by two of the most respected and influential theologians and exegetes of the twentieth century, Bultmann and Barclay, demonstrate

21. Rudolf Bultmann, *Theology of the New Testament*, vol. 1 (New York: Scribner, 1951), 279–80. Italics are in the text.

22. William Barclay, *The Mind of Paul* (London: Collins, 1958), 9.

that the traditional interpretation of Paul in the works of Weber and Bousset continued far beyond the end of the Second World War. The attitude of Jewish scholars in the 1950s also did not shift significantly from the prewar debate. They did not question that Paul was at odds with Judaism. For Samuel Sandmel the starting point was "Paul's personal difficulties with the Law [which] antedate his conversion, rather than follow it."[23] The only thing that could be said in his defense was that Paul "had no sense that he was abandoning Judaism"[24] (even though he did). Paul badly misrepresented rabbinic Judaism because as a Hellenized Jew he possessed only limited knowledge of it.

Even the Dead Sea discoveries had a minor impact on Pauline studies. In 1958 David Flusser suggested that the pre-Pauline tradition could have handed down to Paul some Qumranic elements.[25] The problem was explored with more detail at the end of the 1960s in a collective volume on Paul and Qumran, edited by Jerome Murphy-O'Connor.[26] But the possibility that the Dead Sea Scrolls could have affected, or could shed light on, the core of Pauline theology was not even taken into consideration.

A different line of interpretation began to emerge with William D. Davies's *Paul and Rabbinic Judaism* (1948). Contrary to the common opinion of Jewish and Christian scholars, Davies saw in Paul a rabbinic Jew who did not differ from his fellow Jews except in his belief that the messiah had already come in Jesus.[27] Following this path, the first signs of change came in 1963 with a seminal article by Krister Stendahl, "The Apostle Paul and the Introspective Conscience of the West," in which he pointed out that the traditional Christian view of Paul had more to do with problems

23. Samuel Sandmel, *The Genius of Paul* (New York: Farrar, Straus & Cudahy, 1958), 28.

24. Sandmel, *The Genius of Paul*, 21.

25. David Flusser, "The Dead Sea Sect and Pre-Pauline Christianity," in *Aspects of the Dead Sea Scrolls*, ed. Chaim Rabin and Yigael Yadin (Jerusalem: Hebrew University Press, 1958), 215–66.

26. Jerome Murphy-O'Connor, ed., *Paul and Qumran: Studies in New Testament Exegesis* (London: Chapman, 1968).

27. William D. Davies, *Paul and Rabbinic Judaism: Some Rabbinic Elements in Pauline Theology* (London: SPCK, 1948).

within Christian theology than with the teachings of Paul himself—Paul's major concern was not the weakness of human nature but the salvation of gentiles.[28]

It was not until 1977, however, that a "New Perspective on Paul" began to materialize thanks to the volume *Paul and Palestinian Judaism* by E. P. Sanders. It is hard to overestimate the influence of this volume—a groundbreaking work and a turning point that almost overnight opened a new era in Pauline studies.

Sanders took a quite conservative approach with respect to the trend toward diversity in the study of both Second Temple Judaism and rabbinic Judaism. He still treated Judaism and Christianity as two distinctive systems of religion, which could be monolithically defined and compared.

Sanders's book, however, appeared as a fresh revolution in the field of Pauline studies. It successfully challenged the traditional anti-Judaism of the Lutheran interpretation while reaffirming its principles, *sola gratia* and *sola fides*. The radical opposition between grace and law that made Paul the implacable critic of Jewish legalism was not the authentic voice of the first century but the anachronistic reflection of the controversy that divided Christianity in the sixteenth-century Reformation. Christian theologians no longer needed to denigrate Judaism in order to affirm Christianity, since Judaism also was a religion based on *sola gratia*. Judaism was "covenantal nomism"—a gift of salvation to humankind where works are the condition to remain in the divine covenant established by God's grace, not a means to earn salvation. Paul therefore was completely Jewish in his view of grace and works. The problem, or "what Paul finds wrong in Judaism," was simply that "it is not Christianity."[29] The new covenant in Christ now embraces the whole of humankind and supersedes the old Mosaic covenant, including Jews and gentiles alike through *sola fides* against Jewish ethnocentrism and Jewish national pride.

With the collapse of the "Lutheran" Paul, the myth of the supposed stainless coherence of Pauline thought also began to crumble. Sanders

28. Krister Stendahl, "Paul and the Introspective Conscience of the West," *HTR* 56 (1963): 199–215.

29. Sanders, *Paul and Palestinian Judaism*, 552.

reiterated his view of the unity of Paul's thought: "I do not see any signs of major theological 'development' in Paul's thought. . . . I view Paul as a coherent thinker, despite the unsystematic nature of his thought and the variations in formulation."[30] However, he suggested, Paul was not a systematic theologian. He was a preacher and a minister dealing with communities of flesh-and-blood people who were facing concrete questions and practical problems. For Paul—as Sanders affirmed with effective conciseness—the solution preceded the problem. He saw the gentiles joining Christianity with faith and enthusiasm; his theological effort was to justify the event in retrospect. Paul's argument was not so much the theoretical premise for the entry of the gentiles into the Christian community, but the attempt, albeit a bit confused and theologically not entirely coherent, to justify the event in which he recognized the merciful action of God.

Following this line of reasoning, some scholars and theologians went even further. They insisted on the paradoxical features of Pauline theology: its non-systematic nature, its link to contingent problems and situations, and therefore its substantial inconsistency. Even "the followers of the apostles have hardly ever been able to agree on what he really wanted to say. . . . I can see only one way: Contradiction and tensions have to be accepted as constant features of Paul's theology."[31]

The New Perspective has tried hard to get rid of the most derogatory aspects of the traditional (Lutheran) reading of Paul by claiming that Judaism also should be regarded as a respectable religion based on grace.[32] It has effectively rediscovered the Jewish structure of Paul's thought, emphasizing its pragmatic and pastoral aspects rather than its presumed theological consistency.[33] It has not, however, challenged the view of Paul as the critic of Judaism and the advocate of a new supersessionist model of relations between God and humankind—God's grace "in Christ Jesus" superseded

30. Sanders, *Paul and Palestinian Judaism*, 432–33.

31. Heikki Räisänen, *Paul and the Law* (Tübingen: Mohr Siebeck, 1983), 3, 10.

32. Sidney G. Hall, *Christian Anti-Semitism and Paul's Theology* (Minneapolis: Fortress, 1993).

33. Ben Witherington, *The Paul Quest: The Renewed Search for the Jew of Tarsus* (Downers Grove, IL: InterVarsity Press, 1998).

the Jewish covenant for both Jews and gentiles by creating "one new humanity in place of the two" (Eph 2:13–15). Paul was at odds not with some Jewish groups or some Jewish ideas or practices or "*means* of being properly religious," but with Judaism per se, which he opposed. "Paul's critique of Judaism . . . is neither because of ignorance of the significance of the covenant within Jewish thought nor because of the demise of the covenant conception in late Judaism. *Paul in fact explicitly denies that the Jewish covenant can be effective for salvation, thus consciously denying the basis of Judaism*. . . . Paul polemicizes . . . against the prior fundamentals of Judaism: the election, the covenant, and the law."[34]

Following Sanders, James Dunn and N. T. Wright have also emphasized the contrast between Paul's universalism and Jewish particularism. If Paul misunderstood some elements of his "former" religion, which regrettably fostered anti-Semitic attitudes, then modern Christians should acknowledge and make amends for it. Paul, however, did oppose the standard Jewish view that accepting and living by the law is a sign and condition of favored status (Dunn), as well as the Jewish attachment to a national, ethnic, and territorial identity and to specific boundary-marking behaviors such as circumcision, Sabbath observance, and dietary laws (Wright).[35] In Paul's view, Jesus is and remains the only path to salvation for all humankind.

Two Paths to Salvation?

Sanders's concept of "covenantal nomism" has for some decades dominated Pauline research and the understanding of Second Temple Judaism by New Testament Scholars, no less than Weber and Bousset had shaped the concept of Judaism for previous generations.

Not all scholars, however, were convinced. For some, Sanders went too far in his generous attempt at reconciling Judaism and Christianity. With Stephen Westerholm, they would rather highlight the elements of

34. Sanders, *Paul and Palestinian Judaism*, 551–52. Italics are in the text.

35. See the discussion in John J. Collins, *The Invention of Judaism: Torah and Jewish Identity from Deuteronomy to Paul* (Oakland: University of California Press, 2017), 161.

discontinuity between Paul and Judaism. When purified of its more obvious anti-Jewish excesses, the traditional Augustinian and Lutheran reading is not as removed from the historical Paul.[36]

For other scholars, Sanders did not go far enough in his rediscovery of the Jewishness of Paul. They were more persuaded by Davies's view that Paul was and remained a rabbinic Jew and by Krister Stendahl's remarks that Paul's concern was not individual salvation ("the effect [of the law] upon his conscience") but "the place of the Gentiles in the Church and in the plan of God."[37]

Sanders still saw a radical contraposition between Paul and Palestinian Judaism. For scholars like Lloyd Gaston, Stanley Stowers, and John G. Gager,[38] however, Paul's type of religion was not basically different from anything known from Palestinian Judaism. On the contrary, Paul was and remained a Jew. "Paul never left Judaism, never repudiated Judaism or its law, and never imagined Israel's redemption in terms of Jesus Christ."[39] Paul did not expect Jews to find their salvation through Jesus Christ; all his comments about the law were made in relation to gentiles only: "For Paul, Israel's salvation was never in doubt. What he taught and preached was instead a special path, a *Sonderweg*, for Gentiles."[40] When we have relocated Paul in his proper Jewish setting, "we are left with two basic affirmations: one, God's unshakable commitment to Israel and to the holiness of the Law (=Judaism), and two, the redemption of the Gentiles through Jesus Christ."[41]

Probably no one has followed this line of thought in recent years with more energy, clarity, and coherence than Mark Nanos. In his view Paul is "a Torah-observant Jew . . . a Jew within Judaism, practicing and promoting

36. Stephen Westerholm, *Perspectives Old and New on Paul: The "Lutheran" Paul and His Critics* (Grand Rapids: Eerdmans, 2004); Westerholm, *Justification Reconsidered: Rethinking a Pauline Theme* (Grand Rapids: Eerdmans, 2013).

37. Stendahl, "Paul and the Introspective Conscience of the West," 204.

38. Lloyd Gaston, *Paul and the Torah* (Vancouver: University of British Columbia Press, 1987); Stanley K. Stowers, *A Rereading of Romans: Justice, Jews, and Gentiles* (New Haven: Yale University Press, 1994); Gager, *Reinventing Paul.*

39. Gager, *Reinventing Paul,* x.

40. Gager, *Reinventing Paul,* 146.

41. Gager, *Reinventing Paul,* 152.

a Torah-defined Jewish way of life for followers of Christ."[42] The belief that the messiah has come did not "abrogate" Judaism; on the contrary, "Pauline Judaism" reaffirms the Jews in their practices and beliefs while engaging those who believe in Jesus in a new role "as ambassadors in declaring the reconciliation to the nations."[43] "Bringing non-Jews within Judaism" is in fact the central task of the Jesus movement as a messianic group within Judaism. Non-Jews are not expected to become Jews (proselytes or converts); they are welcome as they are, since the good news is that through Jesus the gates of salvation are now open to non-Jews as well.[44]

Thanks to Nanos's leadership, a new paradigm has emerged today—the "Paul-within-Judaism" perspective, a paradigm that aims to fully rediscover the Jewishness of Paul. Paradoxically, "Paul was not a Christian,"[45] since Christianity, at the time of Paul, did not yet exist as a separate religion from Judaism. The Jesus movement was nothing more than a Jewish messianic movement, and therefore Paul should be regarded as nothing other than a Second Temple Jew and his theology nothing but a form of Second Temple Judaism.

According to Nanos, Paul's letters express "a rhetorical strategy, not a change of halakhic behavior."[46] Nanos shares the point made by Gaston and Stowers[47]—Paul's statements about the law were directed at gentiles practicing or wanting to practice the law, not at Jews. "It was literally a matter of quickly rescuing as many lawless Gentile souls as possible."[48] Paul's anti-Judaism was the result of a misreading of his rhetoric, once the memory of the original Jewish context of his statements was lost in gentile Christianity. "Paul's rhetoric has been traditionally interpreted as a rejec-

42. Mark Nanos, *Reading Paul within Judaism* (Eugene, OR: Cascade Books, 2017), xiii.

43. Nanos, *Reading Paul within Judaism*, 168.

44. See Nanos, *Reading Paul within Judaism*, 127–54.

45. Pamela Eisenbaum, *Paul Was Not a Christian: The Original Message of a Misunderstood Apostle* (New York: HarperOne, 2009).

46. Nanos, *Reading Paul within Judaism*, 26.

47. Gaston, *Paul and the Torah*, 5; Stowers, *A Rereading of Romans*, 21.

48. Stefan Larsson, "Just an Ordinary Jew: A Case Why Paul Should Be Studied within Jewish Studies," *Nordisk Judaistik / Scandinavian Jewish Studies* 29.2 (2018): 9.

tion of Judaism, when what he really meant to clarify was the equal status of the Gentile believers next to their Jewish brethren."[49]

In a field of study where the validity of any approach is immediately assessed also for its contemporary theological implications, the idea of two covenants and two different "ways or paths to salvation, through Christ for Gentiles and through the law for Israel,"[50] has quickly gone beyond the field of academic studies to enter into the contemporary theological debate. It has become popular in Jewish-Christian circles as a convenient way to relate the two sister religions and remove justification for every Christian missionary effort toward the Jews. It has caused some embarrassed reactions by the Christian institutions officially engaged in the dialogue and concerned with its implication for the reading of Paul and Catholic-Protestant relations. In 2015 the Pontifical Council for Promoting Christian Unity felt compelled to issue a statement to reiterate that from the Christian point of view "there cannot be two ways of salvation, since Christ is also the Redeemer of the Jews in addition to the Gentiles."[51]

From a purely historical perspective it should be noted, however, that if the purpose of the two-way solution is to "rehabilitate" Paul from the charge of intolerance, it is not much progress to discover that he was intolerant to all except the Jews.[52] The two-covenant solution may be "a moving attempt to rescue Paul from charges of anti-Judaism and save him from modern Christians,"[53] but what about the Muslims or the believers in other religions or the nonreligious? If salvation to gentiles is offered only in Jesus, gentiles (the overwhelming majority of humankind) remain condemned

49. Larsson, "Just an Ordinary Jew," 7.

50. Gager, *Reinventing Paul*, 59.

51. "The belief of the Church [is] that Christ is the Saviour for all. There cannot be two ways of salvation, therefore, since Christ is also the Redeemer of the Jews in addition to the gentiles. Here we confront the mystery of God's work, which is not a matter of missionary efforts to convert Jews, but rather the expectation that the Lord will bring about the hour when we will all be united." Document by the Pontifical Council for Promoting Christian Unity, December 15, 2015.

52. Kimberly Ambrose, *Paul among Jews: Rehabilitating Paul* (Eugene, OR: Wipf and Stock, 2015).

53. Daniel Boyarin, *A Radical Jew: Paul and the Politics of Identity* (Berkeley: University of California Press, 1994), 42.

unless they believe in Jesus. Even if we remove the Jews from the unbelievers because they keep the torah, are we sure that this was the message that Paul intended to proclaim, that Jesus is the only and exclusive path to salvation for gentiles? Maybe Paul was not anti-Jewish, but if this is what he intended, he remains a champion of religious intolerance.

Paul and Second Temple Judaism

I am a specialist of Second Temple Judaism who sees Christianity and rabbinic Judaism as two parallel (and equally legitimate) outgrowths of the ancient religion of Israel. I look at Paul as the leader of a distinctive Second Temple Jewish movement, which only gradually (long after his time) developed into a separate religion.

I have never been content with the traditional Lutheran approach that makes Paul the divide between Judaism and Christianity. As early as 1991 in *Middle Judaism* I expressed my view that "Paul belongs to Judaism" and denounced the idea of a "universalistic" Christianity emerging from a "particularistic" Judaism as "one of the worst stereotypes of the Christian theological tradition."[54]

My sympathies are all for the Paul-within-Judaism perspective—"Paul was as Jewish as any Jew in antiquity."[55] With deep conviction and no reservations, I would second Mark Nanos in supporting Pamela Eisenbaum's call: "Paul is unambiguously Jewish—ethnically, culturally, religiously, morally, and theologically."[56] What else would he have been? Paul was born a Jew, of Jewish parents, was circumcised, and nothing in his work supports (or even suggests) the idea that he became (or regarded himself as) an apostate.

54. "No New Testament writing is more or less Jewish for the simple reason that they are all Jewish. . . . Even Paul belongs to Judaism: the ideas he expresses (including those that appear most extraneous, such as the theories of original sin and justification by faith), are an integral part of the Jewish cultural and religious patrimony of the first century. . . . Of course, there is an obvious ad extra polemic in the New Testament, but this itself is part of the internal debate within Judaism at the time." Boccaccini, *Middle Judaism: Jewish Thought, 300 BCE to 200 CE* (Minneapolis: Fortress, 1991), 215.

55. Zetterholm, *Approaches to Paul*, 1.

56. Eisenbaum, *Paul Was Not a Christian*, 9.

And yet, as a historian, I am not completely persuaded by the two-path solution. There are exegetical difficulties in the letters of Paul that are hard to overcome. The attempt to dismiss them as mere expressions of "a rhetorical strategy" requires complex and tortured exegesis. The skepticism I share with Second Temple specialists such as Daniel Boyarin and John Collins has even deeper motivations.[57] The two-path solution goes against the results of contemporary research in the field of Christian origins. The Jesus movement was born within Judaism, and the many Jews who joined it (including Paul) did so in their search for salvation. They believed in Jesus as the messiah and accepted baptism for personal reasons that were completely independent from the inclusion of gentiles, before the very idea of a mission to gentiles was even developed.

Paul the Jew

If today we can speak of Jesus the Jew or Paul the Jew, it is because our understanding of Judaism in the first century has profoundly changed in these last few decades. When in 1913, in the introduction to his collection of *The Apocrypha and Pseudepigrapha of the Old Testament*, Robert Henry Charles described Second Temple Judaism as "a church with many parties," he was largely an isolated voice, surrounded by the loudness of normative Judaism and orthodox Christianity.[58] Today this is no longer the case. In the last fifty years critical scholarship has built a solid case about ancient Jewish diversity. The manuscripts of the Dead Sea and the so-called Apocrypha and Pseudepigrapha of the Old Testament reveal a creative and dynamic age and a vital and pluralistic environment in which very different expressions of Judaism coexisted, including the nascent Christian movement.

The term *Judaisms*, coined by Jacob Neusner in the 1980s (and its specular companion *Christianities*) may not have gained universal acceptance,

57. Boyarin, *A Radical Jew*, 42; Collins, *The Invention of Judaism*, 172–73.

58. Robert Henry Charles, ed., *The Apocrypha and Pseudepigrapha of the Old Testament* (Oxford: Clarendon, 1913).

but all contemporary specialists feel compelled to use some form of plural to describe the varieties of Judaism (and Christianity) in the Second Temple period. What once was described as a theological monolith is now commonly presented as the diverse and lively world out of which both Christianity and rabbinic Judaism emerged in a variety of competing expressions.[59]

The obvious reality is before everyone's eyes. There has never been a single moment in the history of Judaism or Christianity in which they have been monolithic religions. Second Temple Judaism was no exception; it was divided into currents of thought in dialogue and competition with each other. Today we speak of Orthodox, Conservative, and Reform Judaism and of Orthodox, Catholic, and Protestant Christianity, but even before these modern divisions emerged, other divisions existed throughout the course of history. Yesterday like today.

Within such a framework, the recognition that Paul was and remained all his life a Jew and a torah-observant Jew cannot be taken as the conclusion of our inquiry; it is only the starting point. Although important in itself, the affirmation of the Jewishness of Paul does not mean much. The real problem, as in the case of Jesus, is not whether Paul was a Jew, but what kind of Jew Paul was, since in the diverse world of Second Temple Judaism, there were many different ways of being a Jew. Labeling Paul as "just an ordinary Jew"[60] may serve as a provocation but is hardly a conclusive answer, as there was nothing like an ordinary Jew in the Second Temple period.

Since many of my remarks in this book focus on the Jewishness of Paul, it is important to clarify, as a premise, what we should not imply by that, in order to avoid some common misunderstandings.

59. I find the semantic discussion on the use of the singular (varieties of Judaism and Christianity) or plural (Judaisms or Christianities) a bit idle. Whether you call them "Judaisms" or "different varieties of Judaism," the substance does not change: in today's time as in the time of Jesus there was not a single way of understanding Judaism but different ways in dialogue or in competition (or Judaisms). And when the movement of Jesus emerged, the very divisions soon became reflected within the new movement, producing different forms of Christianity (or Christianities).

60. Larsson, "Just an Ordinary Jew."

1. In order to reclaim the Jewishness of Paul, we do not have to prove that he was a Jew like everybody else or that he was not an original thinker. It is important not to apply a different standard to Paul than to any other Jew of his time. To claim that finding any idea in Paul that is unparalleled in other Jewish authors makes Paul *non-Jewish* would lead to the paradox that no original thinker of Second Temple Judaism should be considered Jewish—certainly not Philo or Josephus or Hillel or the Teacher of Righteousness, all of whom formulated original answers to the common questions of their age. Why should only Paul be considered non-Jewish or no longer Jewish simply because he developed some original thinking? The very notion of making a distinction within Paul between his Jewish and non-Jewish (or Christian) ideas does not make any sense. Paul was Jewish in his traditional ideas and remained such even in his originality. Paul was a Jewish thinker and all his ideas (even the most nonconformist) were Jewish.
2. In order to reclaim the Jewishness of Paul, we do not have to downplay the fact that he was a very controversial figure, not only within Second Temple Judaism, but also within the early Jesus movement. The classical interpretation that the controversy (both within and outside of his movement) was generated precisely by his obstinate determination to separate Christianity from Judaism does not take into account the diversity of Second Temple Jewish thought. There was never a monolithic Judaism versus an equally monolithic Christianity. There were many diverse varieties of Judaism (including the early Jesus movement, which, in turn, was also very diverse in its internal components).
3. In order to reclaim the Jewishness of Paul, we do not have to prove that he had nothing to say to his fellow Jews and that his mission was aimed only at the inclusion of gentiles. Limiting the entire Pauline theological discourse to the sole issue of inclusion of gentiles would once again confine Paul the Jew to the fringes of Judaism and overshadow the many implications of his theology in the broader context of Second Temple Jewish thought. As Daniel Boyarin has reminded us

> in his work on Paul, a Jew is a Jew, and remains a Jew, even when he or she expresses radical self-criticism toward his or her own religious tradition or against other competing forms of Judaism.[61]

Having clarified these methodological premises, it is possible to attempt to read Paul not simply in relation to Judaism or against his Jewish background but as an integral part of it. Correctly, Pamela Eisenbaum notices that "if a Roman centurion had intercepted Paul's Letter to the Romans he would have quickly spotted it as Jewish. . . . Moreover, Paul's letters would have been regarded as Jewish by other Jews of the time."[62] I would add that if the Jesus movement had never developed as an autonomous religion, this would be still today the way in which we would read Paul—as a Jewish author of the Second Temple period, someone like the Teacher of Righteousness or Philo or Hillel, whose Jewishness has never been questioned in spite of the originality and uniqueness of their positions. There is no need to single out Paul as "a Jew on the margins" or "an anomalous Jew".[63] If we can claim that Philo or the Teacher of Righteousness or Hillel were Jews and at the same time were representatives of distinctive forms of Second Temple Judaism, the same is possible with Paul.

A modern theological reading of Paul cannot of course leave aside the later developments, but a historical, non-anachronistic reading urges us to imagine a time when the Christian Paul was in a situation not different from the Essene Teacher of Righteousness, from the Pharisee Hillel, or from the Hellenistic Jew Philo. Perhaps the time has come for the figure of Paul to be relocated to the original historical context to which he belonged.

There are clear signs that are pushing today in this direction. The most recent dictionaries of Second Temple Judaism, such as the *Eerdmans Dic-*

61. Boyarin, *A Radical Jew*.

62. Eisenbaum, *Paul Was Not a Christian*, 7–8.

63. Calvin J. Roetzel, *Paul: A Jew on the Margins* (Louisville: Westminster John Knox, 2003); Michael F. Bird, *An Anomalous Jew: Paul among Jews, Greeks, and Romans* (Grand Rapids: Eerdmans, 2016).

tionary of Early Judaism or the *T&T Clark Encyclopedia of Second Temple Judaism*, contain articles on Paul.[64] In the same way it includes studies on Qumran or Philo, *4 Enoch: The Online Encyclopedia of Second Temple Judaism* includes Pauline studies.[65] This inclusiveness would have been unthinkable even just a few years ago and coincides with the reappropriation of the nascent Jesus movement to the Judaism of the first century, of which we see significant signals at the international level.[66]

The goal of this volume is to embrace fully the paradigm of the Paul-within-Judaism perspective not as the conclusion but as the starting point of our conversation about Paul. The potential of such an approach has just begun to be manifested. We have still a long way to go before fully understanding all of its monumental implications.

With Gager, I agree that as much as possible "we must resist the temptation to rescue Paul from the embarrassment of contradiction and inconsistency by engaging in tortured exegesis."[67] Before labeling Paul's discourse as incoherent or trying to normalize it because it defies our contemporary categories, we should make every possible effort to understand its internal logic and consistency in its original setting. The authentic Paul must be recovered in his seven authentic letters, but these letters should be read not in splendid isolation from any other Jewish texts of the time but in the context of the entire literature of the period.

We should first try to connect Paul firmly with his Second Temple setting without imposing later categories on him. And we should acquire a better understanding of what it meant to be a follower of Jesus in first-century Judaism. In order to accomplish these goals we should not look at Second Temple Judaism as a static background against which Paul con-

64. John J. Collins and Daniel C. Harlow, eds., *The Eerdmans Dictionary of Early Judaism* (Grand Rapids: Eerdmans, 2010); Loren T. Stuckenbruck and Daniel M. Gurtner, eds., *T&T Clark Encyclopedia of Second Temple Judaism* (London: T&T Clark, 2019).

65. Gabriele Boccaccini, ed., *4 Enoch: The Online Encyclopedia of Second Temple Judaism*, www.4enoch.org.

66. The Enoch Seminar has devoted two international conferences to "Paul the Jew." See Gabriele Boccaccini and Carlos A. Segovia, eds., *Paul the Jew: Rereading the Apostle as a Figure of Second Temple Judaism* (Minneapolis: Fortress, 2016); Isaac W. Oliver and Gabriele Boccaccini, eds., *The Early Reception of Paul the Second Temple Jew* (London: Bloomsbury T&T Clark, 2018).

67. Gager, *Reinventing Paul*, 11.

structed his distinctive system of thought. In history there is no such thing as a movement that suddenly emerges from nowhere, taking a little from everything available in its environment. New, distinctive forms of Judaism emerged dynamically as variants of previous systems, and Paul's Judaism was no exception. We therefore should not start our analysis by defining the theology of Paul, then going backwards from Paul to Judaism in order to understand him. Our starting point should rather be the vibrant intellectual history of Second Temple Judaism going forward to Paul, in order to identify the questions that Paul and the other leaders of the early Jesus movement, and before them Jesus himself, inherited and aimed to answer.

To properly locate Paul the Jew within the diverse world of Second Temple Judaism, we need to establish a better communication between New Testament scholars and Second Temple specialists—two fields of study that, to date, often seem to have remained too distant from and deaf to each other. Not much will be accomplished so long as Pauline specialists discuss Paul only among themselves and Second Temple specialists fail to be engaged in any conversation on Paul. "Pauline studies need Judaic studies" no less than Judaic studies need Pauline studies.[68] The integrity and the future of Pauline studies depend first of all on filling this gap.

Paul the Christian

Once we have firmly reconnected Paul to Judaism, as a Jew among Jews and a Jewish voice in the diversity of Jewish voices of the Second Temple period, it remains the problem of his connection to what we now call Christianity. Obviously, Paul was not a Christian according to the parameters of what Christianity would become in the fourth century or is today.

To say that "Jesus was not the founder of Christianity and Paul was not the second,"[69] however, goes too far. Claiming that Jesus and Paul belong within the context of first-century Judaism in Roman Palestine does not mean that they have nothing to do with the history of later Christianity.

68. See Alan F. Segal, *Paul the Convert: The Apostolate and Apostacy of Saul the Pharisee* (New Haven: Yale University Press, 1990), xiv–xvi; Larsson, "Just an Ordinary Jew," 14.

69. Gager, *Reinventing Paul*, vii.

Making the case that Jesus and Paul should be studied within Judaic studies does not imply that they should no longer be studied also within New Testament and early Christian studies.

In today's world, Judaism and Christianity are in a symmetrical relationship. Judaism and Christianity are two distinct religions. Christianity is not Judaism and Christians are not Jews. In Paul's time, the situation was radically different. Judaism and Christianity were in an asymmetrical relationship. The Jesus movement already existed as a distinct group, but Christianity did not yet exist as a separate religion from Judaism. Most of the Jesus-followers were Jews, as Paul himself was reminded in Jerusalem by the local community: "You see, brother, how many thousands of believers there are among the Jews, and they are all zealous for the law" (Acts 21:20). The Jesus movement was born a messianic and apocalyptic movement within Judaism; it was a variety of Second Temple Judaism.[70]

Being Jewish in the first century did not mean conforming to a monolithic model but engaging in a common debate, in which the categories inherited from the past were played creatively and given continuously new (sometimes unexpected) developments. Being Christian meant being a player in that debate. The Jesus movement was not a foreign body in first-century Judaism, nor was it an illegitimate child of the Jewish tradition.[71]

The relationship between the Jesus-followers and the other Jews worsened over time as soon as the former began to look at themselves not as a particular Jewish group among other Jewish groups but as the only Jewish group that faithfully followed God's will. By the time the Gospel of John was composed, large portions of the Jesus movement had turned into a sect, which viewed their Judaism as the only legitimate form of Judaism.[72] Christianity, however, "never parted" from its Jewish roots.[73] The Jesus movement

70. Gabriele Boccaccini, "What Is Judaism?: Perspectives from Second Temple Jewish Studies." In *Religion or Ethnicity?: Jewish Identities in Evolution*, ed. Zvi Y. Gitelman (New Brunswick: Rutgers University Press, 2009), 24–37.

71. Alan F. Segal, *Rebecca's Children: Judaism and Christianity in the Roman World* (Cambridge: Harvard University Press, 1986).

72. Adele Reinhartz, *Cast Out of the Covenant: Jews and Anti-Judaism in the Gospel of John* (Lanham: Lexington Books-Fortress Academic, 2018).

73. Adam H. Becker, and Annette Yoshiko Reed, eds., *The Ways That Never Parted:*

separated from the other Jewish groups of late antiquity not by the process of rejecting Judaism but by a gradual process of polarization within Judaism.

Neither Jesus nor Paul can be held personally responsible for the separation of Christianity from Judaism, and certainly neither had any intention of promoting a schism. For Paul, the separation between the Jesus-followers and non-believing Jews (what he saw as "a hardening . . . [of] part of Israel") was a painful but temporary incident; in the end "all Israel will be saved" (Rom 11:25–26). However, Paul and Jesus were not completely innocent either. They significantly contributed to triggering the polarization process that resulted in the "parting of the ways" within Judaism between Christianity and Rabbinic Judaism.

The alternative to the traditional Christian Paul who was totally separated from Judaism cannot be a Jewish Paul who is totally separated from Christianity. Paul the Jew should not be seen in contraposition to Paul the Christian. The real Paul belongs neither exclusively to Judaism nor solely to Christianity but rather to the diversity of the Second Temple as one of its most radical and distinctive components. Paul the Second Temple Jew was a first-century Jewish follower of Jesus.

In the diverse world of the Second Temple, being a follower of Jesus was Paul's way of being a Jew and yet contributing to the process of polarization within Judaism that ultimately laid the foundations for the emergence of Christianity as a separate and autonomous religion. Paul the Second Temple Jew belongs synchronically to the history of Judaism as much as he diachronically belongs to the history of Christianity. Paul the Christian and Paul the Jew are one and the same.

Conclusion

The present study does not claim to address all the numerous and complex problems of Paul's theology or discuss the many important contributions

---

Jews and Christians in Late Antiquity and the Early Middle Ages (Tübingen: Mohr Siebeck, 2003).

that so many distinguished scholars have given to the understanding of his life and thought. This is a work of intellectual history aimed to offer some remarks toward a reading of the figure of Paul as one of the major protagonists of Second Temple Judaism, not in spite of but precisely because of the contribution he made to the development of the nascent Jesus movement and of its distinctively Jewish theology. In dealing with a field where every single word of Paul has been subjected to scrupulous and endless scrutiny for centuries, the notes and the bibliography are limited to the essential so as not to lose sight of the main objective of presenting Paul as a Second Temple Jew and a first-century Jewish follower of Jesus. The analysis is conducted in conversation with other international specialists committed to the same goal.

In these past decades the entire discussion seems to have focused on one basic question: whether Paul intended his message of salvation in Christ to be addressed to everyone (Jews and gentiles) or solely to gentiles. Traditionally, Paul is seen as the bearer of a message of salvation offered to Jews first and then to gentiles (an interpretation that the New Perspective has not radically altered). The Paul-within-Judaism perspective has simply restricted the recipients of Paul's message to non-Jews only, at the exclusion of Jews, without significantly altering the contents of his message.

I would like to overcome the current standoff by taking a different direction and questioning some of the shared assumptions of current Pauline research. What was it that Paul and the first followers of Jesus were offering? Salvation in Christ or forgiveness in Christ? And who were meant to be the recipients of the message? All humans (Jews and gentiles), or just the "lost sheep" (i.e., the sinners) of the house of Israel and among the nations? In other terms, what was the good news that the first followers of Jesus (including Paul) were spreading? Salvation by faith for those who believed in Jesus (Jews and gentiles), or forgiveness by faith for the sinners (Jews and gentiles) who believed in Jesus? Was Paul's message a message of damnation for nonbelievers, or a message of rescue for sinners (Jews and gentiles), so "that all shall be saved"?[74]

74. David Bentley Hart, *That All Shall Be Saved: Heaven, Hell, and Universal Salvation* (New Haven: Yale University Press, 2019).

What does the context of Second Temple Judaism tell us about these questions? Paul was a Second Temple Jew and a follower of Jesus, a Jewish thinker and leading exponent of a Jewish reform movement that even in its most radical aspects was an integral part of the Jewish diversity of the first century. Once we cease to superimpose on ancient sources future theological constructs and concerns and stop contrasting Paul the Jew to Paul the Christian, we may even discover that Paul the Jew can help us better understand what the Jesus movement was about and why it emerged as a distinctive form of Judaism before its gradual radicalization caused it to form a separate and autonomous religion.

Chapter 2

Paul the Convert Who Never Converted

Paul the Convert

One of the main foundations of the traditional interpretation of Paul is "a perception of Paul and his communities as something other than Judaism."[1] This idea has remained at the center also of the New Perspective. In the words of N. T. Wright, "being a Jew was no longer Paul's basic identity."[2] Not that anyone ever questioned that Paul was born a Jew, but he converted to Christianity, thus denying the validity of Judaism. From the perspective of later Christianity, his conversion ultimately "transformed [him] into an ex- or even anti-Jew; indeed, into the founder of Gentile Christianity."[3]

Inevitably, any discussion about Paul the Jew must begin with a correct understanding of his supposed conversion. The Pauline Letters and the Acts of the Apostles offer some important information about Paul's life as a Jew before he joined the Jesus movement.

He lived in the Diaspora, as a native and citizen of Tarsus, the capital of the Roman province of Cilicia (Acts 9:11; 21:39; 22:3). In Acts, Paul repeatedly boasts about his status as a Roman citizen, which granted him privileges and protection under Roman Law (Acts 16:22), and he claims to have inherited Roman citizenship from his father ("I was born a citizen," Acts 22:28).

1. Mark Nanos, *Reading Paul within Judaism* (Eugene, OR: Cascade Books, 2017), 15.
2. N. T. Wright, *Paul and the Faithfulness of God* (Minneapolis: Fortress, 2013), 1436.
3. Paula Fredriksen, *Paul the Pagans' Apostle* (New Haven: Yale University Press, 2017), xii.

Born and raised in a Jewish family, since his childhood Paul was presumably a member of the local Jewish community and was instructed in the reading of the torah. He was certainly fluent in both Hebrew/Aramaic and Greek. It seems likely from his writings that he also received a Greek rhetorical education, but no specific reference to it is made in ancient sources.

While there is no doubt that Paul was a Jew from "the tribe of Benjamin" (Rom 11:1; Phil 3:5), the most relevant issue is to understand what kind of Jew Paul was, as there were many different ways to be a Jew in the diverse world of Second Temple Judaism. Here too we have an undisputed answer from ancient sources. Paul calls himself "a Pharisee" (Phil 3:5) as does the Acts of the Apostles (Acts 23:6; 26:5), which also claims that for some time Paul lived in Jerusalem as a pupil of Gamaliel. "I am a Jew, born in Tarsus in Cilicia, but brought up in this city at the feet of Gamaliel, educated strictly according to our ancestral law, being zealous for God" (Acts 22:3). The Letter to the Philippians provides a sort of resume of Paul's early life, before he joined the Jesus movement. Paul refers to himself as being "circumcised on the eighth day, a member of the people of Israel, of the tribe of Benjamin, a Hebrew born of Hebrews; as to the law, a Pharisee; as to zeal, a persecutor of the church; as to righteousness under the law, blameless" (Phil 3:4–6).

Acts 8:1–3 abruptly introduces Paul as an enemy of the church, in stark contrast to the example of the first martyr, Stephen. Paul "approved" of the killing of Stephen and harassed members of the early Jesus movement. He was involved in the persecution against the "church in Jerusalem" that "scattered" the Hellenists "throughout the countryside of Judea and Samaria" (Acts 8:1).

In several cases in his own letters, Paul openly refers to his persecutory actions against the members of the Jesus movement before his "conversion," most significantly in his Letter to the Galatians: "You have heard, no doubt, of my earlier life in Judaism. I was violently persecuting the church" (Gal 1:13). His claim that his persecution resulted from zeal (Gal 1:14; Phil 3:6) seems to indicate that Paul the Pharisee was attracted by the examples of Phinehas or Mattathias, the father of the Maccabees, in their violent struggle against the apostate. Whatever his motives, he joined forces with the high priests—that is, the Sadducees—in their campaign against the most radical members of the Jesus movement.

It should be noted, however, that the persecution in which Paul was involved did not target all members of the Jesus movement but only the Hellenistic party led by Stephen, who according to Acts 7 was charged with promoting radical views about the Jerusalem temple and observance of the torah. The "Hebrews" of the Jesus movement were exempted. Acts 5:34–39 states that Gamaliel played a decisive role in protecting the apostles from the wrath of the Sadducees after the death of Jesus but says nothing about the attitude of the Pharisees toward the Hellenists. As the apostles were Hebrews and not Hellenists, Paul may not have acted in complete contrast with the position of his teacher Gamaliel.

We are told that Paul was then sent to Damascus to investigate the whereabouts of the Jesus-followers there. During his journey to Damascus something happened that radically changed his attitude toward the Jesus movement (Gal 1:13–17; cf. Acts 9:1–19; 22:4–16; 26:9–18). Paul describes the event as "a revelation of Jesus Christ" (Gal 1:12). According to Acts, while "he was going along and approaching Damascus, suddenly a light from heaven flashed around him. He fell to the ground and heard a voice saying to him: 'Saul, Saul, why do you persecute me?'" (Acts 9:3–4).

In the traditional understanding of Paul, the "conversion on the road to Damascus" was the divide between "Paul the Jew" and "Paul the Christian," as Cecily Spencer-Smith Phillimore titled her two novels, respectively in 1927 and 1930, to describe the life of Paul before and after the event.[4] It was at this point, we were told, that Paul ceased to be a Jew and miraculously converted to Christianity. He rejected the legalism and particularism of Judaism and embraced the universal idea of Christianity.[5] Paul the Jew became Paul the Christian by denouncing the wickedness of his early life in Judaism.

4. Cecily Spencer-Smith Phillimore, *Paul the Jew* (London: Hodder and Stoughton, 1927); and *Paul the Christian* (London: Hodder and Stoughton, 1930).

5. Ferdinand Christian Baur, *Paulus der Apostel Jesu Christi: sein Leben und Wirken, seine Briefe und seine Lehre* (Stuttgart: Becher & Müller, 1845; 2nd rev. ed. by Eduard Zeller, 1866–67).

Gentile Proselytes

Conversion as an experience of radical abandonment of one's religious and ethical identity was indeed well known in antiquity. The mixed feelings of excitement and desperation, loss and gain, that accompany the experience of the convert are attested in *Joseph and Aseneth*, in the works of Philo and Josephus, and, in the Greek-Roman context, in the novel *Asinus aureus* ("The Golden Ass") by Apuleius. John Gager and Paula Fredriksen have each demonstrated that in the ancient society, so defined by ethnic boundaries, conversion was much more than "simply a matter of shifting principles or dogmas in one's statement of faith."[6] It was a personally traumatic experience, a total identity transformation characterized by a complete break with the past and the repudiation of family and social ties, especially marked for male converts by the required ritual of circumcision. For Jews it meant accepting a "stranger" as a new family member; to the proselyte's family, he/she was an apostate and a renegade. This was well understood by gentiles, too. "A proselyte, offended patriotic pagans complained, turned his back on family, on ancestral customs, and on the gods."[7] Tacitus felt only contempt for the proselytes because the first lesson they learned was "to despise the gods, to disown their own country and to regard their parents, children, and brothers as of little account" (*Hist.* 5.5.1–2).

Joseph and Aseneth shows that this was exactly what was expected of a convert, male or female.[8] In the mystical frenzy of her conversion, Aseneth undertook an elaborate penitential process:

> Aseneth took all her innumerable gold and silver gods and broke them up into little pieces, and threw them out of the window for the poor and needy. And Aseneth took her royal dinner, even the fatted beasts and the

6. Stefan Larsson, "Just an Ordinary Jew: A Case Why Paul Should Be Studied within Jewish Studies," *Nordisk Judaistik / Scandinavian Jewish Studies* 29.2 (2018): 7; cf. John J. Gager, *Reinventing Paul* (Oxford: Oxford University Press, 2000), 24; and Fredriksen, *Paul the Pagans' Apostle*, 8–31.

7. Fredriksen, *Paul the Pagans' Apostle*, 68.

8. Jill Hicks-Keeton, *Arguing with Aseneth: Gentile Access to Israel's Living God in Jewish Antiquity* (Oxford: Oxford University Press, 2018).

> fish and the meat, and all the sacrifices of her gods, and the wine-vessels for their libations; and she threw them all out of the window as food for the dogs. And after this she took the ashes and poured them out on the floor. And she took sackcloth and wrapped it round her waist, and she removed the fillet from her hair and sprinkled herself with ashes. (Jos. Asen. 10:13–16)

As a result, Aseneth completely broke all ties with her family. Her trust and hope were now only in the God of Israel: "My father and mother denied me, Because I destroyed and shattered their gods; And I have no other hope save in thee, O Lord; For thou art the father of the orphans, and the champion of the persecuted, And the help of them that are oppressed" (12:11).

Resented by their own people, converts were not easily welcomed into their new family, as shown by the second part of *Joseph and Aseneth*, where two of Joseph's brothers, Dan and Gad, plotted with the pharaoh against Aseneth, while the other sons of Jacob defended her. In order to avoid such controversies, later Jewish traditions resolved the problem by making Aseneth a Jew by birth, the daughter of Dinah (Tg. Jonathan on Gen 41:45; 46:20; 48:9; Pirke of Rabbi Eliezer 38:1).

Philo had to face the same prejudices. He also compares proselytes to orphans and widows. They needed special care and protection, because "they have forsaken their country and their national customs in which they were bred up" (*Spec.* 1.309). He reminds his readers that according to the law of Moses, proselytes have now entered the people of Israel as equals, assuming the same normative status as those who were Jewish by birth (Lev 18:26; 19:33–34; Num 15:14–16):

> [Moses] receives all persons of a similar character and disposition, whether they were originally born so, or whether they have become so through any change of conduct, having become better people, and as such entitled to be ranked in a superior class. . . . And these last he calls proselytes, from the fact of their having come over to a new and Godfearing constitution, learning to disregard the fabulous inventions of other nations, and clinging to unalloyed truth. Accordingly, having given equal rank and honor

> to all those who come over, and having granted to them the same favors that were bestowed on the native Jews, he recommends those who are ennobled by truth not only to treat them with respect, but even with especial friendship and excessive benevolence. And is not this a reasonable recommendation? What he says is this. "Those men, who have left their country, and their friends, and their relations for the sake of virtue and holiness, ought not to be left destitute of some other cities, and houses, and friends, but there ought to be places of refuge always ready for those who come over to religion; for the most effectual allurement and the most indissoluble bond of affectionate good will is the mutual honoring of the one God." (*Spec.* 1.51–52)

Although no ancient Jewish text seems to openly promote the conversion of gentiles,[9] the practice was not discouraged, especially for practical purposes in the case of resident aliens, spouses, and slaves. The term *proselyte* appears frequently in Jewish funerary inscriptions and in literary sources (see the reference to "Nicolaus, a proselyte from Antioch" in Acts 6:5). Referring to the Jews of Antioch, Josephus affirms that they not only "multiplied to a great number . . . but they also made proselytes of a great many of Greeks perpetually and thereby, after a sort, brought them to be a portion of their own body" (*J.W.* 7.45).

Jewish Apostates

In addition to examples of non-Jews who converted to Judaism, in ancient sources we have examples of Jews who "removed the marks of circumcision and abandoned the holy covenant. They joined with the Gentiles" (1 Macc 1:15).

Recurrent accusations of apostasy were part of the inner Jewish debate in Second Temple Judaism. These accusations didn't always reflect the will or self-awareness of individuals or groups. Rather, accusations of apostasy

9. Martin Goodman, *Mission and Conversion* (Oxford: Clarendon, 1994), 60–90.

sometimes conveyed only the contempt of religious or political adversaries toward their competitors. Two prominent examples are the invectives of the Qumran community against their religious opponents or the Gospels against other Jews. The Jewish insurgents labeled as "traitors" those who sided with the Romans, only to be repaid with the same accusation by Josephus after he rejoined his former Roman friends, who had been his enemies briefly during the Galilean campaign.[10] Philo thought that the extreme allegorists went too far because they were annulling the practice of the law: "There are some who, regarding laws in their literal sense in the light of symbols of matters belonging to the intellect, are overpunctilious about the latter while treating the former with easy-going neglect" (*Migr.* 89).

These people were not properly apostates. By embracing the "meaning" of the laws they did not intend to abandon Judaism; their goal was rather to interpret its laws, pushing to its ultimate consequences an approach to the law that Philo himself shared and promoted ("It is true that receiving circumcision does indeed portray the excision of pleasure and all passions, and the putting away of impious conceit," *Migr.* 92).

However, in some cases it seems clear that some Jews really intended to renounce their own Jewish ethnic identity. The descendants of Alexander, son of Herod the Great, whom the Romans made rulers of the Armenian kingdom, "soon after their birth, deserted the Jewish religion, and went over to that of the Greeks" (Josephus, *Ant.* 18.141). Their decision (or their family's decision) was apparently for opportunistic reasons, as a way to facilitate their careers within the Roman administration. In *Moses* 1.30–31, Philo criticizes those who, unlike Moses, in their search for social success "overlook their relations and friends, and transgress the laws according to which they were born and brought up; and they overturn their national hereditary customs to which no just blame whatever is attached, dwelling in a foreign land, and by reason of their cordial reception of the customs among which they are living, no longer remembering a single one of their ancient usages."

10. Pierre Vidal-Naquet, *Flavius Josèphe; ou, Du bon usage de la trahison* (Paris: Éditions de Minuit, 1977).

This appears to have been also the case of Philo's nephew, Tiberius Julius Alexander, the Jewish governor of Judah and Egypt, who according to Josephus "was not abiding by his ancestral customs" (*Ant.* 20.100). Tiberius, however, in his life maintained friendly relations with fellow Jews and continued to be involved in Jewish affairs through his close relationship with Herod Agrippa II and Berenice. More difficult to penetrate are the motivations of Antiochus, whose story Josephus tells in the seventh book of the *Jewish War.* "Antiochus [was] one of the Jewish nation and greatly respected on account of his father, who was the governor of the Jews at Antioch" (*J.W.* 7:47). At the beginning of the Jewish War, perhaps in an attempt to save himself from the impending disaster, he became the accuser of his own people. "In order to give a demonstration of his own conversion and of his hatred of the Jewish customs, he offered sacrifices after the manner of the Greeks" (*J.W.* 7.50). This is the behavior not of a person who aimed to promote an alternative view of being Jewish but rather of someone who wanted to show that he was no longer a Jew.

A Move within Judaism

At the time of Paul, there were indeed gentile-born proselytes who joined Judaism and Jewish-born apostates who abandoned Judaism. But this was not the experience of Paul. It is not simply that Paul "had no sense that he was abandoning Judaism" (even though he ultimately did), as Samuel Sandmel believed.[11] The idea that Paul abandoned Judaism when he "converted" to the Jesus movement is overtly anachronistic. It took only one sentence for Pinchas Lapide to dismiss it, by revealing the naked truth: "Paul did not become a Christian, since there were no Christians in those times."[12]

The Jesus movement in the first century was a Jewish messianic movement, not a separate religion. Paul, who was born and raised a Jew, remained such after his "conversion"; nothing changed in his religious, ethi-

11. Samuel Sandmel, *The Genius of Paul* (New York: Farrar, Straus & Cudahy, 1958), 21.

12. Pinchas Lapide and Peter Stuhlmacher, *Paul: Rabbi and Apostle* (Minneapolis: Augsburg, 1984), 47.

cal, and cultural identity. "Are they Hebrews? So am I. Are they Israelites? So am I. Are they descendants of Abraham? So am I" (2 Cor 11:22).

Talk about a transition from one religion to another is therefore in the case of Paul "totally inappropriate"[13] and "misleading."[14] As Mauro Pesce rightly observed, "Paul never converted. . . . He never used the Greek word *metanoia* or the verb *metanoein* to define his own change of life. . . . Paul was not an apostate. . . . Paul lived and interpreted the experience of revelation that changed his life as an event internal to his Jewish experience. . . . The revelation he received in no way attenuated his Jewish identity and even less abolished it or put it in crisis. . . . Paul was and remained only Jewish."[15] The language of conversion should be abandoned, once and for all.

In search of an alternative model to explain Paul's experience, scholars have tried to relate it to other categories. Following Gager ("The model of a conversion within a religious tradition is clearly more appropriate than any other"),[16] Nanos correctly talks of a choice within Judaism: "Believing that Jesus was the Messiah and affiliating with other Jews who shared that conviction involved making a choice between different groups of Jews, but the choices were within Judaism, they did not signify leaving the practice of a Jewish way of life."[17] Paul's experience should be understood not as a chapter in the parting of the ways between Christianity and Judaism but as an incident in the context of the diversity of Second Temple Judaism.

A Call, Not a Conversion

Some scholars today prefer the language of Stendahl that Paul was "called rather than converted."[18] In the words of Pamela Eisenbaum, Paul was a

13. Lloyd Gaston, *Paul and the Torah* (Vancouver: University of British Columbia Press, 1987), 6.

14. Gager, *Reinventing Paul*, 24.

15. Mauro Pesce, *Le due fasi della predicazione di Paolo. Dall'evangelizzazione alla guida delle comunità* (Bologna: Dehoniane, 1994), 13–32. Translation is mine.

16. Gager, *Reinventing Paul*, 25.

17. Nanos, *Reading Paul within Judaism*, 32.

18. Krister Stendahl, *Paul among the Jews and Gentiles* (Minneapolis: Fortress, 1976).

Jew "called by God to fulfill a particular mission, one that was foretold in the Hebrew prophets: to bring knowledge of the one God—the God of Israel—to all the nations of the world."[19]

That "Paul understood the essential content of his conversion to be his mission to the Gentiles"[20] is not just an inference of modern scholars. In the Letter to the Galatians, Paul himself claims that the mission to the gentiles had a central role in his conversion: "God, who . . . called me through his grace, was pleased to reveal his Son to me, so that I might proclaim him among the Gentiles" (Gal 1:15–16). In his self-understanding, Paul's mission as an apostle to the gentiles was a divine call (Rom 1:1–6; 11:13).

The emphasis on the future mission of Paul to gentiles also plays an important role in the narratives of Acts, where it is said that Jesus himself introduced Paul to Ananias "in a vision" as "an instrument whom I have chosen to bring my name before Gentiles" (Acts 9:10–15).

However, saying that nothing else changed in the life of Paul (and in his religious beliefs) would be equally misleading.

First of all, while it is true that Christianity did not yet exist as a separate religion from Judaism, the Jesus movement already existed as a distinctive group within Judaism. In no way should we minimize the relevance of the event. In describing his experience as not so much a (prophetic) "call" but rather as an (apocalyptic) "revelation" (Gal 1:12), Paul himself indicated the radicality of the event. Paul did not abandon Judaism but moved from one variety of Judaism to another.

Today if a Reform Jew becomes an ultraorthodox Jew, or vice versa, many would also be tempted to describe this experience in terms of conversion, although this is certainly not the appropriate term. Similarly, Paul's conversion was not a conversion into another religion but a move within Judaism, and yet it was a no less dramatic experience. It reoriented Paul's entire life and worldview and changed his understanding of Judaism. It implied a radical reassessment of what it meant to be a Jew: "Whatever gains I had, these I have come to regard as loss because of Christ. More

19. Pamela Eisenbaum, *Paul Was Not a Christian: The Original Message of a Misunderstood Apostle* (New York: HarperOne, 2009), 3.

20. Gager, *Reinventing Paul*, 27.

than that, I regard everything as loss because of the surpassing value of knowing Christ Jesus my Lord. For his sake I have suffered the loss of all things, and I regard them as rubbish" (Phil 3:7–8).

Secondly, Paul did not understand the message of Jesus as one addressed exclusively to the gentiles but rather as the same message addressed first to the Jews and then presented to the gentiles. "I had been entrusted with the gospel for the uncircumcised, just as Peter had been entrusted with the gospel for the circumcised (for he who worked through Peter making him an apostle to the circumcised also worked through me in sending me to the Gentiles)" (Gal 2:7–8).

This is also the picture presented in Acts, where Paul preaches before gentiles and kings, as well as before the people of Israel (Acts 9:15). Consistently, the narrative of Paul's conversion (first announced by Jesus himself to Ananias and the Jesus believers of Damascus, 9:1–19) is repeated by Paul twice in Acts: the first time (in Aramaic) to the people of Israel ("brothers and fathers," 22:1–16) in Jerusalem and then to King Agrippa II and Berenice and the Roman governor Festus in Caesarea (26:9–18).

According to Acts, Paul's first mission was to his fellow Jews: "Immediately he began to proclaim Jesus in the synagogues." No gentiles were involved. He "confounded the Jews who lived in Damascus by proving that Jesus was the Messiah" (Acts 9:20–22).

In the narrative of Acts but also in the autobiography of Galatians, many years passed between the time Paul was called and the time when his mission to the gentiles began. The revelation he received on the road to Damascus did not immediately make him the apostle to the gentiles but a follower of Jesus.

Second Temple Judaism was divided into many groups. Many of the first (Jewish) members of the new movement came from other Jewish groups, within which they had been raised and to which they were more or less closely affiliated. In the Acts of the Apostles we notice the tendency to continue to identify members of the Jesus movement according to their former affiliations.

The Hellenists (like Stephen and his companions), as opposed to the Hebrews, were those who came from Hellenistic-Jewish communities (Acts

6:1–6). Acts 15:5 defines as belonging "to the sect of the Pharisees" those followers of Jesus who at the so-called Council of Jerusalem promoted the view that to be saved, the baptized gentiles should "be circumcised and ordered to keep the law of Moses." Interestingly, Paul is not reckoned among them but among their most strenuous opponents (Acts 15:12).

It is true that both in his letters and in the Acts of the Apostles, Paul refers to himself as a Pharisee especially in relation to the doctrine of resurrection. Modern scholars, starting with Henry Thackeray,[21] have highlighted numerous "Pharisaic" elements in Paul's theology. However, after receiving "the revelation of Jesus Christ" Paul identified no longer with the Pharisaic movement but instead with the Jesus movement. Paul did not remain a Pharisee with sympathies for the Jesus movement. He joined the new movement and became one of its leaders. As soon as Paul joined the Jesus movement he became a *former* Pharisee. Being a former Pharisee, however, does not mean that Paul repudiated each and every doctrine of the Pharisees. In particular, eschatological ideas such as the end of time, the coming of the messiah, the resurrection of the dead, and the last judgment would always remain at the center of his thought.

Being a former Pharisee did not make Paul a former Jew. There is no anti-Judaism in Paul. To say that Paul was anti-Jewish would be like saying that Martin Luther was anti-Christian. Luther was anti-Catholic, he even referred to the Pope as the anti-Christ. But Luther was not anti-Christian. He was against Roman Catholicism, not against Christianity. He did not view Protestantism as the replacement of Christianity, but as the summit and true form of Christianity.

Likewise, the presence of controversies against other Jewish groups does not make Paul a former Jew and anti-Jewish. Paul's Christianity was a form of Judaism and his letters are Second Temple Jewish documents. Paul did not repudiate Judaism; he only opposed other competing forms of Judaism. He did not view the Jesus movement as the replacement of Judaism but as the summit and true form of Judaism.

21. Henry St. John Thackeray, *The Relation of St. Paul to Contemporary Jewish Thought* (London: Macmillan, 1900).

Paul was not an apostate and enemy of Judaism, nor a schizophrenic personality in whom the Christian and the Jewish identities struggled to assert themselves against each other. Paul's Christianity was Paul's Judaism—Paul's idea of Judaism. That God might have "rejected his people" never crossed Paul's mind (Rom 11:1). Paul was not an illegitimate child of Judaism but a sibling who argued with his siblings.

Conclusion

Paul never converted. He was a Jew *before* his "conversion" and remained such *after* his "conversion." He was born, lived, and died as a Jew. Paul should never be labeled as a former Jew or a former member of the Jewish people. His "transformative experience" of revelation radically changed his life and his way of understanding Judaism,[22] but it should never be referred to as a conversion. By switching his loyalty from the Pharisaic party to the Jesus movement, Paul did not lose any of his Jewishness but remained within the boundaries of Second Temple Jewish diversity.

In Paul's time, the group of Jesus followers was not a separate religion but a Jewish messianic movement. What does it mean exactly? It would be simplistic to reduce the early Christian message to a generic announcement about the imminent coming of the kingdom of God and about Jesus as the expected messiah. Likewise, it would be simplistic to imagine Paul as simply a Pharisee to whom the name of the future messiah was revealed and who now believed himself to be living in the end of time.

Paul was not "a Rabbinic Jew who differed from the rest of rabbinic Judaism only in thinking that the Messiah had come," as William D. Davies concluded.[23] He was a Pharisee who joined "a new apocalyptic, Jewish sect."[24]

22. Laurie Anne Paul, *Transformative Experience* (New York: Oxford University Press, 2014).

23. See E. P. Sanders, *Paul and Palestinian Judaism: A Comparison of Patterns of Religion* (London: SCM, 1977), 11.

24. Alan F. Segal, *Paul the Convert: The Apostolate and Apostacy of Saul the Pharisee*

Before being known as the apostle to the gentiles, Paul became a member of the Jesus movement. He then gradually characterized his apostolate within the Jesus movement with a particular emphasis on the mission to gentiles. Before Paul the apostle to the gentiles, there was Paul the Jesus-follower. Paul's belief in Jesus did not make him less Jewish but did radically reorient his view of Judaism. An investigation about Paul cannot, therefore, avoid the questions of what the early Jesus movement was about in the context of Second Temple Judaism, what it meant for a Jew like Paul to join the Jesus movement, and what it meant for "many thousands" of Jews like Paul (Acts 21:20) to recognize Jesus as the messiah and be baptized "in the name of Jesus Christ" (2:38).

(New Haven: Yale University Press, 1990), 6. Even though I think that the terms "convert" and "conversion" are not appropriate, I agree with the substance of Segal's position: Paul was a Pharisee who "converted" within Judaism to an apocalyptic form of Judaism.

Chapter 3

Paul the Apocalyptic Jew

The Apocalyptic Worldview of Paul the Jew

There is growing attention among scholars to the apocalyptic framework of Paul's thought. In the words of Paula Fredriksen, Paul lived in "a Jewish world incandescent with apocalyptic hopes."[1] It was Paul's firm belief that his time was history's final hour. Most of Paul's moral statements make no sense except in a context of imminent eschatology. As Paul states, "the appointed time has grown short. . . . The present form of this world is passing away" (1 Cor 7:29–31). His mission to the gentiles was directly inspired by his conviction of living near the "end," which is the time of the restoration of Israel and of the inclusion of the nations.

At any time, Paul expected that God would put an end to this world (1 Thess 1:10; 5:3). To the Thessalonians he repeats his conviction that "we who are alive" will experience "the coming of the Lord" (1 Thess 4:15–17). And to the Romans he reiterates that with each passing day the end is closer: "You know what time it is, how it is now the moment for you to wake from sleep. For salvation is nearer to us now than when we became believers; the night is far gone, the day is near!" (Rom 13:11–12).

However, eschatological expectations about the end of time, the coming of the messiah, the last judgment, and other future events related to

1. Paula Fredriksen, *Paul the Pagans' Apostle* (New Haven: Yale University Press, 2017), xii.

that time, such as the restoration of Israel and the inclusion of non-Jews, are not sufficient to explain all aspects of Paul's apocalyptic thought.

The letters of Paul are rife with references to superhuman evil powers. "The god of this world" (2 Cor 4:4), of "the present evil age" (Gal 1:4b), is the devil, the rebellious angel whom Paul calls "Satan" (Rom 16:20) or "Beliar" (2 Cor 6:15). His dominion, however, is nearing its end: "The God of peace will shortly crush Satan under your feet" (Rom 16:20), a phrase that echoes God's curse of the serpent and God's promise to Eve's offspring (Gen 3:15). Paul clearly sees the end of time as a battle against cosmic evil forces: "Then comes the end, when [Christ] hands over the kingdom to God the Father, after he has destroyed every ruler and every authority and power. For he must reign until he has put all his enemies under his feet. The last enemy to be destroyed is death" (1 Cor 15:24–26). In Romans he describes the entire creation "groaning in labor pains" and longing to "be set free from its bondage to decay" (Rom 8:18–25).

New Testament scholarship (starting from Ferdinand Christian Baur) has long downplayed these references as inconsequential for the understanding of Paul's broader theology. Specialists such as Julius Wellhausen dismissed apocalypticism as one of the theological degenerations of "late" Judaism: "Apocalyptic suggests armchair speculation, sectarian rigidity, egocentric particularity, ethical passivity, and an adherence to an obsolete world view and to misleading language that cannot and should not be resuscitated."[2]

Only a few scholars, notably R. H. Charles, took seriously the relevance of the Jewish apocalyptic worldview (or at least some apocalyptic tendencies in Second Temple Judaism) for the comprehension of Christian origins.[3] Even fewer were those who considered Paul's apocalyptic categories worthy of study[4] or adhered to Albert Schweitzer's conclusion

2. See N. T. Wright, *The Paul Debate: Critical Question for Understanding the Apostle* (Waco, TX: Baylor University Press, 2015), 136.

3. R. H. Charles, *Religious Development between the Old and the New Testaments* (London: Williams & Norgate, 1914).

4. Otto Everling, *Die paulinische Angelologie und Dämonologie: ein biblisch-theologischer Versuch* (Göttingen: Vandenhoeck & Ruprecht, 1888); Richard Kabisch, *Die Eschatologie des Paulus in ihrer Zusammenhangen mit dem Gesamthegriff des Paulus* (Göttingen: Vandenhoeck & Ruprecht, 1893).

that "being-in-God is for Paul impossible so long as the angelic beings still possess some kind of power over man. . . . In general, the view of Jewish eschatology is that the evil of the world comes from the demons. . . . In its simplest form the conception of redemption is that the Messianic Kingdom puts an end to this condition."[5]

According to Rudolf Bultmann, apocalyptic categories ought to be "demythologized" because they are "incredible for modern man, for he is convinced that the mythical view of the world is obsolete."[6] Bultmann intended to reject the means more than the content of the ancient apocalyptic message, yet his stance also contributed to the general dismissal of Jewish apocalypticism as an outdated mythological worldview.

The old bias of New Testament scholarship against Jewish apocalypticism is still apparent in Sanders's claim that "the similarity between Paul's view and apocalypticism is general rather than detailed. Paul did not . . . calculate the times and seasons, he did not couch his predictions of the end in visions involving beasts, and he observed none of the literary conventions of apocalyptic literature."[7]

The "rediscovery" of apocalypticism, pursued in the 1970s and 1980s by scholars such as Klaus Koch, Walter Schmithals, Paul Hanson, Christopher Rowland, and John Collins[8] has restored dignity to the field and inspired a new generation of Pauline specialists who have looked at the apocalyptic elements in Paul as key elements of his theology.

Directly inspired by these studies, an interpretative school emerged that placed the "apocalyptic Paul" at the center of its own reflection. Schol-

5. Albert Schweitzer, *The Mysticism of Paul the Apostle* (London: Adam and Charles Black; New York: Holt, 1931), 3, 55. German ed.: *Die Mystik des Apostels Paulus* (Tübingen: Mohr Siebeck, 1930).

6. Rudolf Bultmann, *Kerygma and Myth* (1953; New York: Harper and Row, 1961), 3.

7. E. P. Sanders, *Paul and Palestinian Judaism: A Comparison of Patterns of Religion* (London: SCM, 1977), 542.

8. Klaus Koch, *Ratlos vor der Apokalytik* (Gütersloh: Gütersloher Verlagshaus Gerd Mohn, 1970); Walter Schmithals, *Die Apokalyptik: Einführung und Deutung* (Göttingen: Vandenhoeck & Ruprecht, 1973; Paul D. Hanson, *The Dawn of Apocalyptic: The Historical and Sociological Roots of Jewish Apocalyptic Eschatology* (Philadelphia: Augsburg, 1975); Christopher Rowland, *The Open Heaven: A Study of Apocalyptic in Judaism and Early Christianity* (London: SPCK; New York: Crossroad, 1982); John J. Collins, *The Apocalyptic Imagination: An Introduction to the Jewish Matrix of Christianity* (New York: Crossroad, 1984).

ars such as J. Christiaan Beker and J. Louis Martyn have argued that at the core of Paul's message is the "triumph of God over the forces of evil,"[9] that salvation in Paul is more a corporate matter than an individual problem, and that the gospel of Paul is first of all a message of liberation from the power of evil: "Jesus' death . . . is oriented not toward personal guilt and forgiveness, but rather toward corporate enslavement and liberation."[10]

The apocalyptic worldview is not in Paul a mythological accessory that can be easily isolated and set aside; it is the essential framework that shapes all aspects of Paul's theology, every single problem that Paul addresses in his letters or discusses with his readers.

"The genesis of Paul's apocalyptic . . . lies in the apostle's certainty that God has invaded the present evil age by sending Christ and his spirit in it."[11] Paul discerns three heavenly actors: God, the messiah, and "supra-human powers other than God" who fight for control of creation. This world has fallen under the dominion of evil forces. The Christ-event is God breaking into this world and restoring God's rule over the world and over the evil powers controlling it. Paul finds himself at the juncture of the two ages, a unique moment in history when the Christ-event has already disarmed the powers of evil though it has not destroyed them completely. Although Satan and evil powers have been judged in Jesus's death and resurrection, for Paul such forces remain at work in the present age with residual but deleterious power against the people of God until their definitive destruction in the last judgment.

The studies of the apocalyptic Paul school are a reminder that whatever problems Paul was addressing in his letters, they must be understood within the dualistic framework of Jewish apocalypticism. In Paul's view, the problem of individual salvation has cosmic implications and cannot be separated from a collective dimension.

9. J. Christiaan Beker, *Paul's Apocalyptic Gospel: The Coming Triumph of God* (Philadelphia: Fortress, 1982); J. Louis Martyn, *Galatians*, Anchor Bible 33A (New York: Doubleday, 1997); see also Richard Bell, *Deliver Us from Evil: Interpreting the Redemption from the Power of Satan in New Testament Theology*, WUNT 216 (Tübingen: Mohr Siebeck, 2007).

10. Martyn, *Galatians*, 101.

11. Martyn, *Galatians*, 98.

The Origin of Evil in Jewish Apocalypticism

Recent research on Jewish apocalypticism has confirmed that for many Second Temple Jews the central concern was indeed the problem of liberating the cosmos from the power of evil caused by superhuman agents.[12] Apocalypticism was a complex worldview. It was not a generic expectation of a better future. It addressed, first of all, the problem of the superhuman origin of evil. The eternal peace promised in the world to come was viewed as the reversal of the current situation of corruption and decay and the restoration of the original goodness of the universe, disrupted by the angelic sin. Eschatology was not born of hope for a better future or optimism in the progress of humankind; it was the product of pessimistic protology.

We are unfortunately so much influenced by later Christian speculations about the original sin that we may not be willing to recognize the Second Temple Jewish roots of such a concept for fear of transferring back Christian ideas to ancient Jewish sources. From texts such as 1 Enoch, Daniel, and Jubilees, however, we know that in Second Temple Judaism there was a heated debate on the origin of evil. In apocalyptic circles many viewed the origin of evil not as a consequence of God's will or human transgression but as a rebellion of superhuman angelic powers.

"A master narrative is the foundational story in a larger community. . . . A counterstory is a story that contests the world view of the master narrative, not by trying to erase the narrative itself, but by making significant changes in its literary web. The result is that the new restored narrative communicates something entirely different."[13] The apocalyptic "counterstory" of the Book of the Watchers focuses on the collapse of the creative

12. Paolo Sacchi, *Jewish Apocalyptic and Its History* (Sheffield: Sheffield Academic Press, 1996); Gabriele Boccaccini, *Roots of Rabbinic Judaism: An Intellectual History, from Ezekiel to Daniel* (Grand Rapids: Eerdmans, 2002); Miryam T. Brand, *Evil Within and Without: The Source of Sin and Its Nature as Portrayed in Second Temple Literature* (Göttingen: Vandenhoeck & Ruprecht, 2013).

13. Helge S. Kvanvig, "Enochic Judaism—a Judaism without the Torah and the Temple?" in Gabriele Boccaccini and Giovanni Ibba, eds., *Enoch and the Mosaic Torah: The Evidence of Jubilees* (Grand Rapids: Eerdmans, 2009), 164; cf. H. Lindemann Nelson, *Damaged Identities, Narrative Repair* (Ithaca, NY: Cornell University Press, 2001), 6–20, 150–88.

order by a cosmic rebellion (the oath and actions of the fallen angels). Against the idea of stability and order conveyed in the "master narrative" of the Mosaic torah, the Enochians argued that God's order was no more, having been replaced by the current disorder: "The whole earth has been corrupted by Asael's teaching of his [own] actions; and write upon him all sin" (1 En. 10:8). In the Enochic interpretation, the rebellion of the "sons of God" was not simply one of the primeval sins that characterized the ancient history of humankind; it was the mother of all sins, the original sin that corrupted and contaminated God's creation and from which evil relentlessly continues to spring forth and spread. By crossing the boundaries between heaven and earth, the rebellious angels destroyed the divisions set by God at the time of creation. The consequent unleashing of chaotic forces condemns humans to be victims of an evil they have not caused and cannot resist.

Despite God's reaction and the subsequent flood, the divine order of creation was not restored. The cosmos has not returned to what it was. The good angels, led by Michael, defeated the evil angels, led by Shemihazah and Asael (Azazel); however, the victory resulted not in the death or submission of the rebels but in their confinement "in the wilderness which was in Dudael," where the fallen angels were imprisoned "in a hole . . . underneath the rocks of the ground" (1 En. 10:4–6, 11–12). The mortal bodies of the giants, the offspring of the evil union of immortal angels and mortal women, were killed (1 En. 10:9–10); however, their immortal souls survived as evil spirits and continue to roam about the world (1 En. 15:8–10). Humankind was decimated with the flood but not annihilated, as Noah's family survived (1 En. 10:1–3). Creation was cleansed but not totally purified, as God used water and not the "fire" that is reserved only for "the great day of judgment" (1 En. 10:6). However disturbing this idea may be, God's reaction limited but did not eradicate evil. The world is still dominated by evil forces. A time of "seventy generations" was set "until the eternal judgment is concluded" (1 En. 10:12).

Enochic Judaism first introduced into Judaism the concept of the "end of days" as the time of final judgment and vindication beyond death and history. What in the prophetic traditions was the announcement of an indeterminate intervention of God became in the Enochic tradition the expectation of a final cataclysmic event that will mark the end of God's "first" creation and the beginning of a "second" creation—a new world qualitatively different from, and discontinuous with, what was before. Apocalyptic eschatology arose from protology.

Enochic Judaism and the Mosaic Torah

How the doctrine of the superhuman origin of evil relates to the individual search for salvation and human freedom is one of the crucial questions in the analysis of ancient Jewish apocalypticism. The absence of any specific reference to the legal material in the Mosaic torah has led Second Temple specialists, including John Collins, to talk of Enochic Judaism as a "non-Mosaic" form of Judaism.[14] Does "non-Mosaic," however, mean anti-Mosaic? Scholars are divided about the actual attitude of Enochic Judaism toward the torah. At one extreme, Paolo Sacchi claimed that "the lack of any mention . . . of the Torah in the Enochic literature cannot be regarded simply as an omission. The Enochians never accepted the Torah of Moses."[15] George Nickelsburg also once referred to "Enochic Wisdom" as "an alternative to the Mosaic Torah."[16] On the other hand, E. P. Sanders viewed it as a system compatible with "covenantal nomism."[17]

It is true that the revelation to Enoch was claimed to precede that of Moses and was in no way subordinated to it. However, at no point in the Enoch texts do we see evidence of controversies against the Mosaic torah. The most explicit reference to the torah is in the Apocalypse of Weeks,

14. John J. Collins, *The Invention of Judaism: Torah and Jewish Identity from Deuteronomy to Paul* (Oakland: University of California Press, 2017).

15. Luca Arcari, "The Book of the Watchers and Early Apocalypticism: A Conversation with Paolo Sacchi," *Henoch* 30.1 (2008): 9–79 (quot. 23).

16. George W. E. Nickelsburg, "Enochic Judaism: An Alternative to the Mosaic Torah," in *Hesed Ve-Emet: Studies in Honor of Ernest S. Frerichs*, ed. Jodi Magness and Seymour Gitin, BJS 320 (Atlanta: Scholars Press, 1998) 123–32.

17. E. P. Sanders, *Paul and Palestinian Judaism: A Comparison of Patterns of Religion* (London: SCM, 1977).

where it is presented as a gift given by God in the "fourth week" as "a law for all generations" (1 En. 93:6), a precious gift destined to last forever. The law is listed along with the First Temple as a remedy established by God to limit the spread of evil.

Enochic Judaism's problem with the Mosaic torah did not derive from a direct criticism of the law but was the product of protology. It came from the recognition that the angelic rebellion had made it difficult for people to follow any laws (including the Mosaic torah) in a universe now disrupted by the presence of superhuman evil. The problem was not the torah itself (its divine origin is never questioned or dismissed) but the difficulty human beings have in doing good deeds, which affects the human relationship to the Mosaic torah. The shift in focus was not primarily from Moses to Enoch but from the trust in human responsibility to the drama of human culpability and guilt. While at the center of the Mosaic torah was the human responsibility to follow God's laws (as exemplified by the experience of Adam and Eve in the garden of Eden), at the center of Enochic Judaism was now a paradigm of victimization of all humankind.

Nowhere, however, do Enochic texts deny human freedom or exonerate humans from the consequences of their transgressions. In the Enochic tradition evil affects human choice, but "lawlessness was not sent upon the earth, but man created it by themselves, and those who do it will come to a great curse. . . . All your unrighteous deeds are written down day by day, until the day of your judgment" (1 En. 98:4–8). The purpose of the myth of the fallen angels was to absolve God from responsibility for a world that the Enochians deemed evil and corrupted. It was not intended to deny human accountability. In the Enochic system of thought the two contradictory concepts of human responsibility and human victimization had to coexist between the Scylla of an absolute determinism and the Charybdis of an equally absolute anti-determinism. Accept either of these extremes and the entire Enochic system would collapse into the condemnation of God as the unmerciful source of evil or the unjust scourge of innocent creatures.

This is why it would be incorrect to talk of Enochic Judaism as a form of Judaism "against" or "without" the torah. Enochic Judaism was not "competing wisdom" but, more properly, a "theology of complaint." There was no alternative Enochic *halakhah* for this world, no Enochic purity code, no Enochic torah. All hope of redemption was postponed to the end of time; this world is ruled by evil forces. And yet, regardless of how hard it might be, in the judgment humans will be accountable according to their deeds. The Enochians were not competing with Moses—they were merely complaining.

An Apocalyptic Debate (Dream Visions, Daniel, and Jubilees)

Consistent with the previous Enochic tradition, the Animal Apocalypse in the book of Dream Visions describes the entire course of history as a continuous process of degeneration that started at the beginning of humankind with the angelic sin. Humans were created as "white-snow cows" (1 En. 85:3), but then "a star fell down from heaven and managed to rise and eat and to be pastured among those cows" (86:1). The fall of the devil was followed by a large rebellion of angels: "Many stars descended and cast themselves down from the sky upon that first star, and they became bovids among those calves and were pastured together with them" (86:2). As a result, new animal species were born ("elephants, camels, and donkeys," 86:4). Neither the intervention of the good angels, who reduce the rebels to impotence (87–88), nor the flood (89:2–8) can eradicate evil from the earth. Evil descendants are bound to arise, even from the holy survivors. From Noah, "the snow-white cow which became a man" (i.e., like the angels), "three cows" are born, but "one of those three cows was snow-white, similar to that [first] cow [Shem], and one red like blood [Japheth], and one black [Ham]. . . . They began to bear the beasts of the fields and the birds. There arose out of them many [different] species" (89:9–10).

History thus witnesses a continuous expansion of evil, with no way for human beings to oppose its spread. Nobody is spared: in the metaphorical world of the Animal Apocalypse, even the Jews, who are the noblest part of humankind, carry the evil gene of degeneration; by the generation of Jacob, from "cows" they have become "sheep." Within this framework, there is no room for any reference to the Mosaic torah. Its presence does not alter the progressive spread of evil. In particular, after the Babylonian exile the situation collapses; God entrusts God's people to "seventy shepherds" (angels), who show themselves to be evil, breaching their assigned tasks in such a way that the entire history of Israel in the postexilic period unfolds under a demonic influence (see 1 En. 89:59–70). Reconstructed "under the seventy shepherds," the Second Temple can only be a contaminated sanctuary. "They again began to build as before; and they raised up that tower which is called the high tower, and they placed a table before [the tower], but all the bread which was upon it was polluted and impure" (1 En. 89:73). This situation of evil and decay is irremediable and will end only with the establishment of a "new creation" at the end of time, when God's intervention restores the goodness of the universe. In the insurgency of the "white sheep" in his own time, the apocalyptic author saw a sign that the end was imminent.

The Enochic view had disturbing implications for the self-understanding of the Jewish people as the people of the covenant. In the Book of Dream Visions, the chosen people of Israel are promised future redemption in the world to come, but in this world, Israel is affected by the spread of evil without any divine protection, as are all other nations.

This view that made the chosen people almost defenseless before evil was not universally shared within Judaism. Many (like the Pharisees and the Sadducees) apparently rejected the very idea of the superhuman origin of evil. Other paths were pursued in order to save human freedom and God's omnipotence—paths that led to alternative solutions, from the *cor malignum* of 4 Ezra to the rabbinic *yetzer hara.*[18] All had in common the attempt to subordinate the origin of evil to God's will and deny the presence of the devil as the ruler of this world. Even within apocalyptic circles, among those who shared the principle of the superhuman origin of evil, there were competing theologies.

Daniel has often, and sometimes improperly, been associated with Dream Visions. The two documents are nearly contemporaneous, both

18. Ishay Rosen-Zvi, *Demonic Desires: Yetzer Hara and the Problem of Evil in Late Antiquity* (Philadelphia: University of Pennsylvania Press, 2011); Matthias Henze and Gabriele Boccaccini, eds., *4 Ezra and 2 Baruch: Reconstruction after the Fall* (Leiden: Brill, 2013).

being dated to the first years of the Maccabean revolt, between the murder of Onias III, the last legitimate Zadokite high priest (170 BCE), and the death of Antiochus Epiphanes (164 BCE). Both documents are apocalyptic; they share the same literary genre (apocalypse) and the same worldview (apocalypticism), and—even more significant—substantially address the same questions. However, as all specialists now agree, Daniel does not come from the same circles that produced the Books of Enoch.

Like Dream Visions, the book of Daniel presents Israel in exile and under God's wrath, and at the center of a cosmic battle between good and evil. And yet Daniel does not condemn the temple or the former priestly ruling class but instead even lavishes some praise on the last legitimate Zadokite high priest Onias III. Both texts support the Maccabean insurgency, and yet the attitude of these two apocalyptic texts toward the revolt is distinctively different. The Enochic writing is more militant, while Daniel leans toward "passive resistance." Not surprisingly, their respective attitudes toward the Mosaic torah is also different. In chapter 9 Daniel explicitly refers to the "law of Moses" and makes it one of the concurring reasons for the spread of evil, which is not attributed only to the presence of superhuman forces and cosmic conflicts but also to human transgression. "The curse and the oath written in the law of Moses, the servant of God, have been poured out upon us, because we have sinned against [him]" (Dan 9:11).

The length of the punishment and the presence of evil are explained and calculated with categories that are compatible with the torah of Moses, with Leviticus in particular: "If you will not obey me . . . I will set my face against you, and you will be struck down by your enemies. . . . If in spite of these punishments you have not turned back to me, but continue hostile to me, then I too will continue hostile to you: I myself will strike you sevenfold for your sins" (Lev 26:14–24). This is exactly what happened according to Daniel 9. Israel broke the covenant (Lev 26:15) and was punished by God with seventy years of exile, as announced by the prophet Jeremiah, yet despite this Israel did not turn back to God but continued its hostility. As a result, God multiplied the punishment "sevenfold" and the "seventy years" prophesied by Jeremiah became "seventy weeks" of years (Dan 9:24).

This difference of attitude within the apocalyptic tradition between the Enochic and Danielic streams was crucial in the Hasmonean and Roman periods, generating (increasingly) different and distinctive positions toward the Mosaic torah.

Meanwhile, a third position emerged. In the mid-second century BCE, the book of Jubilees reacted against this demise of the covenantal relation with God by creating an effective synthesis between Enoch and Moses that many scholars see as the decisive step in the foundation of the Essene movement.[19]

Like the Enochians, the Essenes were an apocalyptic movement that shared the superhuman origin of evil and proclaimed themselves the champions of the poor against the well-to-do.[20] Their roots were in the same traditions of dissent that had challenged the power of the Zadokite priesthood. They never showed any nostalgia for the time when the House of Zadok was in power, nor did they do anything intended to restore their authority. In a supersessionist mood they even referred to themselves as the true "sons of Zadok," just to demonstrate that they (and not the evil high priests of the House of Zadok) were the ones referred to and prophesied by Ezekiel.

If the book of Jubilees was—as seems likely—at the foundation of the entire Essene movement, the text that inspired the ideological revolution from which both "orders" of the Essenes came, the *yahad* and the "camps" described in the Damascus Document,[21] then there was something very substantial that the entire Essene movement did not like in the Enochic movement—the idea that the Jews, like the other nations, were defenseless against the power of evil. It was against the Enochic lack of hope and initiative in this world that the book of Jubilees reacted by creating an original synthesis between Enoch and Moses. This synthesis can no longer be labeled as either Enochic or Mosaic but is now distinctively Essene.

19. See Boccaccini and Ibba, eds., *Enoch and the Mosaic Torah*; and James C. VanderKam, *Jubilees: A Commentary* (Minneapolis: Fortress, 2018).

20. John J. Collins, *Apocalypticism in the Dead Sea Scrolls* (London: Routledge, 1997).

21. John J. Collins, *Beyond the Qumran Community: The Sectarian Movement of the Dead Sea Scrolls* (Grand Rapids: Eerdmans, 2010).

The Essenes rejected the idea that the sin of angels had undermined the election of Israel. They maintained that the election of Israel was established by God at creation (Jub. 2:21). The distinction between Jews and gentiles does not belong to the (corrupted) history of humankind but to the (uncorrupted) order of creation. The effectiveness of the covenant was not diminished by the fall of angels. The power of the evil spirits was limited, and the sons of Noah were given a "medicine" that protects them from evil (10:10–14). This does not mean that the people of Israel were completely safe in a world now dominated by evil. It remained safe only so long as they kept the boundaries that separated them from the other peoples. The issue of observing the right *halakhah* became central to preserving the holiness of the people.

Out of this concern, the Essenes became more and more skeptical of the effectiveness of the Mosaic torah. They believed that the Mosaic *halakhah* was "incomplete." The complete torah was written only on the tablets of heaven and was revealed only partially in the Mosaic torah. Moses, like other mediators such as Enoch and his successors, was only given a glimpse of the tablets of heaven. In this regard, as Collins states, "Jubilees, which retells the stories of Genesis from a distinctly Mosaic perspective, with explicit halachic interests,"[22] stands in stark contrast to the Enochic tradition. The merging of Mosaic and Enochic traditions establishes a space in which the people of Israel can now live protected from the evil of the world under the boundaries of an alternative *halakhah*. No longer a "theology of complaint," Essenism now offered a competing view of the heavenly law and its interpretation.[23]

The movement that sprang from the book of Jubilees, while reiterating the Enochic concept of the superhuman origin of evil, took a different trajectory than that of the Enochic tradition, a trajectory that in some sectarian texts leaned dangerously toward predeterminism.[24] The parting of the ways between the Essene movement and Enochic Judaism is confirmed

22. John J. Collins, "How Distinctive Was Enochic Judaism?," *Meghillot: Studies in the Dead Sea Scrolls* V–VI (2007): 17–34.

23. Gabriele Boccaccini, "From a Movement of Dissent to a Distinct Form of Judaism: The Heavenly Tablets in Jubilees as the Foundation of a Competing Halakah," in Boccaccini, and Ibba, eds., *Enoch and the Mosaic Torah*, 193–210.

24. Armin Lange, *Weisheit und Prädestination: Weisheitliche Urordnung und Prädestination in der Textfunden von Qumran* (Leiden: Brill, 1995).

by the autonomous developments of the Enoch literature (Epistle of Enoch and the Parables of Enoch), independent of the Essene movement.[25]

Contrary to what we see in Jubilees, the Halakhic Letter, or the Community Rule, Enochic Jews would never develop an alternative *halakhah* and would never question the legitimacy of the Mosaic torah. They kept their focus on the difficulty humans have in obeying the torah as a consequence of the spread of evil. Enochic Judaism was born as, and always remained, a "theology of complaint."

To sum up: at the turn of the Common Era, we have evidence of at least three distinct apocalyptic responses. They all shared the idea of the superhuman origin of evil, but each offered a slightly different relationship to the Mosaic torah.

(a) The Enochic trajectory ignored the Mosaic torah not because it had something against it, but because its focus was entirely on the difficulty of humans (Jews and gentiles alike) to obey the torah.
(b) The Essene trajectory created an alternative *halakhah* as the only effective protection for the Jews against the evil world and condemned non-Jews as hopelessly at the mercy of evil forces.
(c) Finally, the Danielic trajectory seemed to offer the possibility of a rapprochement between apocalyptic and covenantal elements and a greater role for the Mosaic torah.

As a Pharisee, Paul had strong eschatological expectations. He would have shared Daniel's prophecies about the end of time, the resurrection of the dead, and the last judgment, but he would have also firmly rejected the cosmic dualism of Jewish apocalypticism. By joining the Jesus movement, he made a decisive and uncompromising choice of field within Second Temple Judaism. He bound himself to a conceptual framework—that is, the apocalyptic concept of the superhuman origin of evil—that, although susceptible to variations, forced his reflection into precise boundaries and separated him from the Pharisaic tradition.

25. Gabriele Boccaccini, *Beyond the Essene Hypothesis: The Parting of the Ways between Qumran and Enochic Judaism* (Grand Rapids: Eerdmans, 1998).

To treat the apocalyptic elements in Paul as a sort of cultural relic of no relevance, which could be conveniently set aside, dismissed, or ignored without altering the general structure of his thought, generates a schizophrenic understanding of Paul. It artificially separates Paul's meditation on the power of sin from its original Second Temple Jewish setting as well as from the common conversation within the early Jesus movement. These apocalyptic elements are the premise and the center of Paul's thought. All other elements, individual and collective, are subordinated to Paul's central apocalyptic idea of the superhuman origin of evil, including the problem of personal salvation, the inclusion of non-Jews, and the relevance of the Mosaic torah.

Conclusion

Before Paul the apostle to the gentiles we have Paul the Jesus-follower. As a result of the revelation he experienced on the road to Damascus, Paul did not abandon Judaism but fully embraced the Jewish apocalyptic worldview of the early followers of Jesus, centered on the idea of the superhuman origin of evil, the corruption of the universe, and the expectation of the end of time. Paul the Pharisaic Jew became Paul the apocalyptic Jew. Whatever message he delivered in his letters, it cannot be separated from the cosmic and dualistic context in which it was originally framed.

To complicate the picture, the Jesus movement was not only a Jewish apocalyptic movement but also a Jewish messianic movement. Paul adhered to a form of apocalyptic Judaism where the ancient ideas about the corruption of the universe and the expectations of the end had already merged with speculations about the manifestation of God's messiah. The early followers of Jesus claimed that the messiah had already come and that his coming had something to do with the cosmic battle between good and evil. The end was the time of the final confrontation between God's messiah and the ruler of this age, Satan. Without a correct understanding of the encounter between apocalypticism and messianism it is impossible to have a correct understanding of Paul's thought.

Chapter 4

Paul the Messianic Jew

Trajectories of Ancient Jewish Messianism: From Historical to Eschatological

The messianic idea is so much ingrained in the Jewish and Christian traditions as to make it difficult even to imagine a time when it was not, at least in the forms familiar to us. For Jews and Christians today, the messianic idea is closely linked to the idea of the end of time and the new creation, but these concepts emerged only at a relatively late stage in the development of the Jewish religion. At its inception, the messianic idea in Israel had only a historical, not eschatological, meaning and resulted in the hope for political and religious leaders and guides. Messianic expectation in ancient Israel remained "relatively modest in their claims for the future king" even when the messianic hope took the shape of the expectation of a miraculous future of peace and comfort. Under the influence of Egyptian ideas of kingship, the messiah was given superhuman features and a special parent-child relationship with God as his "beloved son."[1] The ancient messiahs of Israel were initially the kings and afterward the priests, who during the Second Temple period assumed the king's role and functions. The anointing was the sign of the mission they had been entrusted by God. Messianic functions could also be metaphorically attributed to non-Jewish figures, as in the famous

1. Adela Yarbro Collins and John J. Collins, *King and Messiah as Son of God: Divine, Human, and Angelic Messianic Figures in Biblical and Related Literature* (Grand Rapids: Eerdmans, 2008), 15.

case of King Cyrus celebrated by Deutero-Isaiah as the messiah who freed Israel from the yoke of Babylon (Isa 45:1–7).

The transition from old to new forms of royal messianism is still apparent in Flavius Josephus. Like an ancient prophet of Israel, Josephus proclaimed the Roman Emperor Vespasian the new messiah. "I am here to announce to you a brighter future. . . . You, Vespasian, will be Emperor and Caesar, you and your son. . . . You, Caesar, you are not only my Master, but also the owner of the land, the sea and all humankind" (*J.W.* 3.400–402). Thanks to this "prophecy," Josephus was able to account for his own failure as a general, save his own life, and earn for himself a respectable name (Flavius) and a respectable future as friend of the emperor.[2] Josephus's "prophecy" would leave a mark on the history of the Roman Empire itself. The Roman historian Suetonius reports:

> It was confirmed in all the Orient an old and constant belief: that by order of the Fates the one who at that time had come from Judea would obtain the universal lordship. The Jews referred to themselves the prediction that, as later events would show, concerned a Roman emperor in Judea. . . . When [Vespasian] consulted the oracle of God at Carmel, the fates were so reassuring to promise that he would have been anything (no matter how great) he thought and contemplated. One of the noble prisoners, Josephus, when he was put in chains, with great insistence asserted that he would soon be freed by [Vespasian] once he had become Emperor. (*Vita Vespasiani* 4.5; 5.6)

The "prophet" Josephus, however, also knew a different kind of messiah. In his view the homage paid to Vespasian was only a convenient and temporary truce; it did not preclude the hope that in the future another, more powerful messiah would arise to redeem Israel and free the people from the yoke of foreign domination. In reporting Daniel's vision of a great image, consisting of a head of gold, shoulders and arms of silver, belly and

2. Pierre Vidal-Naquet, *Flavius Josephe; ou, Du bon usage de la trahison* (Paris: Minuit, 1977).

thighs of bronze, and legs and feet of iron, Josephus places great emphasis, more so than in the original, on the reference to the "stone" broken off from a mountain, which "fell upon the image and overthrew it, breaking it into pieces and leaving not one part of it whole. So that the gold and silver and bronze and iron were made finer than flour, and when the wind blew strongly, they were caught up by its force and scattered abroad; but the stone grew so much larger that the whole earth seemed to be filled with it" (*Ant.* 10.207, cf. Dan 2:31–35).

Josephus was aware that he had entered a minefield—the succession of empires was a very delicate subject to which both Jews and Romans were equally sensitive. He had to be very careful to avoid any explicit reference to eschatological expectations that might echo the fundamentalism of the Zealots and their critique of the status quo and the authority of his Roman patrons. He thus couches his discussion in a thread of subtle allusions. As recognized by most modern commentators, Daniel's four kingdoms originally were, in order, the Babylonians, the Medians, the Persians, and finally, the Greeks.[3] That Josephus had in mind a different order is immediately evident by the explanatory notes he added to the original text. The first empire, we are told, is "Babylon," which "will eventually be brought to the end by two kings" (Josephus aggregated Medians and Persians as the second empire). The second empire in turn "will be destroyed by another king from the West" (here the allusion is clearly to Alexander the Great [cf. 1 Macc 1:1–9] and clearly precludes the interpretation that the third empire could be the Persian empire). Finally, to dominate for a long time will be a fourth empire, which has all the features of power and strength of the Roman Empire but whose identity is not revealed explicitly (*Ant.* 10.208–209).

Caught between patriotic pride and Realpolitik, Josephus spoke a coded language, which he knew could be understood only by his Jewish readers. He wanted to deliver hope without creating dangerous illusions, to foster national pride without alarming and offending the Romans. This explains the total absence of any reference to the "weakness" inherent in the "mixed" nature of the fourth empire, which was an important element

3. John J. Collins, *Daniel: A Commentary* (Minneapolis: Fortress, 1993).

in Daniel's vision, and in Josephus is instead replaced by the reference (both praising and threatening) to the superiority of its "iron nature . . . harder than that of gold, or silver or bronze" (*Ant.* 10.209). As for the "stone"—which in Daniel was a symbol of "a kingdom that shall never be destroyed, nor shall this kingdom be left given to another people" (Dan 2:44)—Josephus remains silent, taking refuge behind a comfortable, and somewhat convenient, self-censorship. "Daniel also revealed to the king the meaning of the stone, but I have not thought it proper to relate this, since I am expected to write of what is past and done and not of what is to be; if, however, there is anyone who has so keen a desire for exact information that he will not stop short of inquiring more closely but wishes to learn about the hidden things that are to come, let him take the trouble to read the book of Daniel, which he will find among the sacred writings" (*Ant.* 10.210).

This comment would seem to signal the end of the discourse, but it does not. Josephus later informs his reader that the prophecy of Daniel about the "stone" has not yet been accomplished but belongs to the future. Reiterating that Daniel "not only foretold things to come as the other prophets, but also marked the time in which it would take place," Josephus adds that "while the other prophets foretold disaster . . . Daniel was a prophet of happy events" (*Ant.* 10.267–268). We thus learn that the prophecy of the "stone" points not only to a future event, intended to be accomplished at an unspecified time, but to an event that will bring "joy" for Israel. A few pages later, at the conclusion of his presentation of the figure of Daniel, Josephus informs the reader—as if everybody knew it—that the prophet "also wrote about the Roman Empire, that Jerusalem would be taken by them and the temple destroyed (by them)" (*Ant.* 10.276), although we are not told how or when. When the reader takes all these elements together, it is not difficult to fully understand all the political implications of Josephus's interpretation of Daniel. The succession of the "four empires" includes the Romans; they will be the most powerful rulers of all and "will dominate for a long time" but not forever. The "stone"—which Josephus sees as the symbol par excellence of a messianic king of the everlasting kingdom—cannot therefore refer to Vespasian. Vespasian was indeed a "messiah," but in him the Jewish messianic expectations were not completely fulfilled.

Eschatological Messianism in the Second Temple Period

By the turn of the common era, several Jewish circles had gone beyond the expectation of human messiahs and had embraced the (then highly controversial) notion of the end of time and the beginning of a new creation. The collapse of the Hasmonean monarchy and the beginning of Roman rule had contributed to the idea that the restoration of Israel was not destined to happen in this world but in a world to come.[4]

It was not, however, the result of a linear process of development. Jewish society during the Second Temple period remained divided into many groups characterized by many different theologies. This complexity was also reflected in the existence of diverse messianic expectations. Even among those who sustained the expectation of eschatological messianism, there were different opinions about the identity, nature, and functions of the eschatological messiah. Different theologies produced different forms of eschatological messianism. These differences were competitive and exclusive and cannot be traced back to a single framework.[5]

Given his special role at the end of time, the eschatological messiah was imagined as being more powerful than any historical messiah. Existing sources allow us to reconstruct two major models, respectively defined by the terms "Son of David" and "Son of Man."

The Messiah "Son of David"

Proto-rabbinic traditions viewed evil as a consequence of human transgression and looked forward to an eschatological future in which God would restore his kingdom and Israel would cease to be "punished" by foreign domination and regain its sovereignty under the leadership of a righteous

4. John J. Collins, "Il messia Figlio di Davide nel giudaismo del Secondo Tempio alla luce dei manoscritti di Qumran," in *Il messia tra memoria e attesa*, ed. Gabriele Boccaccini (Brescia: Morcelliana, 2005), 49–67.

5. Jacob Neusner et al., eds., *Judaisms and Their Messiahs at the Turn of the Christian Era* (Cambridge: Cambridge University Press, 1987).

king. The king messiah would be the Son of David, the heir of the dynasty to whom God promised eternal power.

These ideas found their fullest expression for the first time in the first century BCE, in the so-called Psalms of Solomon, and are echoed in the "Son of God" texts from Qumran.[6] The primary task of the messiah Son of David would be the redemption of Israel. "See, Lord, and raise up for them their king, the Son of David, to rule over your servant Israel in the time known to you, O God. Undergird him with the strength to destroy the unrighteous rulers and purge Jerusalem from nations that trample her to destruction" (Pss. Sol. 17:21–22). The Son of David is a powerful ruler, invested by God with an extraordinary mission, yet he is a human messiah, "anointed" just as his ancestor, David, was anointed as a boy by Samuel (1 Sam 16:1–13). Psalm 17 opens, culminates, and ends with the exaltation of the supreme and eternal worship of God; God is "our king" (Pss. Sol. 17:1, 46) and "his [i.e., the messiah's] king" (17:34). The messiah is the leader and deliverer of Israel, and wise ruler of the people (Pss. Sol. 17:26), but he is not a personal savior. If so, God would incomprehensibly duplicate what he has done on Sinai. The righteousness of the individuals (including the messiah) rests in their obedience to "the law that God has commanded so that we might live" (Pss. Sol. 14:3) and that the messiah will enforce rigorously. "And he will be a righteous king over them, taught by God. There will be no unrighteousness among them in his days, for all shall be holy and their king shall be the Lord Messiah" (Pss. Sol. 17:32).

The messiah is thus confined to a marginal role in relation to the centrality of the torah, which is the sole and exclusive means of salvation that God in God's justice and mercy has given to free and responsible humankind so that they can learn how to turn their actions to good according to God's will. God alone is the Judge. "Our works are the fruit of our choice and the ability of our souls, to do right and wrong in the works of our hands. In your righteousness you oversee human beings. The one who does what is right saves up life for himself with the Lord, and the one who does what is wrong causes his own life to be destroyed" (Pss. Sol. 9:4).

6. Yarbro Collins and Collins, *King and Messiah*, 48–74.

Royal messianism and centrality of the law are the two pivotal ideas around which the entire messianic reflection of the proto-rabbinic traditions developed in the Second Temple period. At the end of the first century CE, the association between the doctrine of the four kingdoms of Daniel and the idea of the King Messiah was fulfilled. Like Josephus, 2 Baruch gives the fourth kingdom the features of Rome, without any weakness. "His dominion will be harder and worse than those that were before him and will rule for many times" (2 Bar. 39:5). And the "rock" (or "Son of Man") of Daniel has lost its original symbolic or angelic features; it is now the king messiah, the anointed one of the eschatological times.

> And it will happen when the time of the fulfillment [of the fourth kingdom] is approaching in which it will fall, that at that time the dominion of my Anointed One . . . will be revealed. . . . The last ruler who is left alive at that time will be bound, whereas the entire host will be destroyed. And they will carry him on Mount Zion, and my Anointed One will convict him of all his wicked deeds . . . and will kill him and protect the rest of my people who will be found in the place I have chosen. And its dominion will last forever until the world of corruption has ended and until the times which have been mentioned before have been fulfilled. (2 Bar. 39:7–40:3)

The same elements are found in the later Targum Neofiti.[7] The fourth kingdom, which will come after "Greece," is obviously Rome, "Edom, the evil [kingdom] that will fall and not rise again" (Tg. Neof. Gen 15:12; cf. Tg. Neof. Deut 32:24). The destruction of the fourth kingdom will be the work of the King Messiah. "From the house of Jacob shall arise a king. He will destroy those who are guilty from the sinful city, namely, Rome" ([Tg. Neof.] Frg. Tg. Num 24:19). This king is the Davidic messiah from the House of Judah, an invincible warrior, ruthless in vengeance, but also a righteous king and ruler of a kingdom of peace and prosperity.

7. See Miguel Pérez Fernández, *Tradiciones mesiánicas en el Targum Palestinense* (Valencia: Institución San Jerónimo, 1981).

> From the house of Judas . . . is the king, to whom sovereignty belongs and to whom all kingdoms will submit. How beautiful is the King Messiah who will rise from the children of Judah! He will gird the loins and fight against his enemies and kill kings and princes. He will redden the mountains with the blood of the slain, and whiten the hills with the fat of their warriors. . . . How beautiful [are] the eyes of the King Messiah, more than pure wine! He does not use them to see the nakedness or the shedding of innocent blood. His teeth are whiter than milk, because he does not use them to eat the products of violence and robbery. The mountains will redden with the vineyards and the wine presses, and the hills will whiten with the abundance of wheat and herds of small cattle. (Tg. Neof. Gen 49:10–12)

It is equally interesting to notice what these texts on the Son of David say and do not say. They do say that the king messiah is the protagonist of the collective redemption of Israel; but the messiah has no role in the salvation of the individual, which is exclusively governed by the law, the centrality of which increases in proportion to the removal of any hopes for an immediate end of Roman domination. The torah is the only hope of salvation; it is the foundation on which the faith in the coming of the messiah springs forth, *spes contra spem*, even in the hardest times. The failure, one after another, of all alternative proposals (including the hope in the imminent coming of the messiah) paradoxically served the purposes of a school of thought that since its inception aimed to make the torah central to the life of Israel and could now triumphantly proclaim its uniqueness as the only remaining hope in times of despair. This is what 2 Baruch said after the destruction of the temple: "The shepherds of Israel have perished, and the lamps which gave light are extinguished, and the fountains from which they used to drink have withheld their streams. . . . But shepherd and lamps and fountains came from the Law and when they go away, the Law will abide. . . . Now that Zion has been taken away from us, we have nothing apart from the Mighty One and his Law. . . . There is one law by One, one world and an end for all those who exist" (2 Bar. 77:13, 15; 85:3, 14).

This explains the caution with which the Mishnaic tradition welcomed messianic expectations. It certainly agrees with them (see m. Ber. 1:5), yet its major concern was to subordinate any eschatological hopes to the centrality of the torah. "Anyone who accepts the yoke of the law is free from the yoke of the state and from the yoke of the world. But the one who is subtracted from the yoke of law, is subject to the yoke of the state and the world" (m. Abot 3:5). It was only within the boundaries of such a conceptual framework, and with clear limitations (in a condition of "probation" and subordination to the torah), that the figure of the "king messiah" emerged and became normative in rabbinic Judaism.

The Messiah "Son of Man"

Within the vast constellation of apocalyptic movements (and in particular within its Enochic stream), the problem of salvation was complicated because of the belief in the doctrine of the superhuman origin of evil.[8] What was needed was liberation not only from the nations, to whom Israel was subjected because of its sins, but also from the forces of evil that govern this world. The need for a heavenly messiah was born from this need to fight not only against the rulers of this world but also against Satan and his heavenly hosts, who are the lords of the lords of this world. Since the bearers of evil on earth come from heaven, and no mortal could ever subdue them, it follows that the messiah also should come from heaven to be stronger than his opponents.[9]

In the Book of Parables of Enoch (also composed in the late first century BCE) the "Son of Man," the archangel Michael of Daniel's vision, becomes a different kind of celestial figure, a judge who will reveal himself at the end of time.[10] He will then "sit on the throne of glory and will judge Azazel and his followers and his army, in the name of the Lord of Spirits" (1 En. 55:4). Created at the beginning of the first creation before the angelic

8. Gabriele Boccaccini, *Roots of Rabbinic Judaism: An Intellectual History, from Ezekiel to Daniel* (Grand Rapids: Eerdmans, 2002).

9. Paolo Sacchi, "Messianism," chapter 14 of *The History of the Second Temple Period* (Sheffield: Academic Press, 2000), 380–408.

10. See Sabino Chialà, *Libro delle Parabole di Enoc* (Brescia: Paideia, 1997); Gabriele Boccaccini, ed., *Enoch and the Messiah Son of Man: Revisiting the Book of Parables* (Grand Rapids: Eerdmans, 2007); George W. E. Nickelsburg and James C. VanderKam, *1 Enoch 2: Book of Parables, Book of the Luminaries* (Minneapolis: Fortress, 2012).

hosts, the Son of Man is a preexistent, superhuman being, destined to remain "hidden" until his glorious manifestation.

> At that hour, that Son of Man was given a name, in the presence of the Lord of the Spirits, the Before-Time; even before the creation of the sun and the moon, before the creation of the stars [i.e., the angels], he was given a name in the presence of the Lord of the Spirits. He will become a staff for the righteous ones in order that they may lean on him and not fall. He will be the light of the gentiles and he will become the hope of those who are sick in their hearts. . . . He was concealed in the presence of [the Lord of the Spirits] prior to the creation of the world, and for eternity. (1 En. 48:2–6)

There are therefore "two powers in heaven";[11] this is how the Book of Parables explains the mysterious reference to the "thrones" in the vision of Daniel (Dan 7:9). The Son of Man is not subject to divine justice; he is the author of judgment, the judge "seated on the throne of glory" (1 En. 69:29) to the right of the Most High, and as such he is, like God, worthy of honor and glory and worship. Divine features and functions are attributed to the figure of the messiah, so prominently that the authority of the messiah mingles with the authority of the supreme God and the messiah also becomes an object of veneration, in heaven as well as on earth. "All who dwell upon the earth shall fall and worship before him; they shall glorify, bless and sing the name of the Lord of spirits" (1 En. 48:5). And yet there is a clear distinction between God and the Son of Man in the Parables of Enoch; the former is the creator and the latter is created.

What Kind of Messiah Was Jesus?

Scholars struggle to reconstruct the messianic message of the historical Jesus, and it is virtually impossible to penetrate his messianic self-

11. Alan F. Segal, *Two Powers in Heaven: Early Rabbinic Reports about Christianity and Gnosticism* (Leiden: Brill, 1977).

consciousness. Jesus left no writings, nor are there any contemporaneous reports of his preaching; we must rely only on the post-factum testimony of his followers. Everything we know about the historical Jesus, however, "the origin of [his] activity in the apocalyptic movement of John the Baptist, the known events of his life, and the apocalyptic movement initiated by his followers after his death suggest that Jesus understood himself and his mission in apocalyptic terms."[12]

Many of Jesus's sayings indicate a clear prophetic self-consciousness on the part of the teacher from Nazareth. Some of these sayings are recognized as perhaps the most authentic expressions of the teaching of the historical Jesus, such as when he expressed his disappointment to his hometown ("Prophets are not without honor, except in their hometown, and among their own kin, and in their own house," Mark 6:4) or his prescient lament over Jerusalem ("Jerusalem, Jerusalem, the city that kills the prophets and stones those who are sent to it!" [Matt 23:37; Luke 13:34]). There is no doubt, however, that the tendency of the Christian tradition (perhaps as early as the time of Jesus) was to attribute to the teacher and prophet from Nazareth a very special relationship with God the Father and superhuman features and functions from the very beginning. In the narratives of Jesus's baptism and transfiguration, a voice from heaven proclaims, "You are my Son, the Beloved; with you I am well pleased" (Mark 1:11; cf. 9:7). Those who see in Jesus "one of the prophets," or the redivivus John the Baptist or Elijah, are contrasted with Peter and his profession of faith: "You are the Messiah" (Mark 8:28–29). In essence, for his first followers, Jesus was more than a righteous prophet; he was the Righteous One, and as the eschatological messiah, he was not just a son of God but the beloved Son of God.

The relative absence of explicit messianic statements by Jesus is not surprising. In the diverse world of Second Temple Judaism, the term *messiah* was an extremely vague and ambiguous term. The primary need and challenge for any messianic pretender in the first century was rather to clarify the characteristics of his messianic claims. It then becomes even more relevant that Jesus was assigned only sayings that related him to the Enochic Son of

12. Collins, *King and Messiah*, 171.

Man. The only case in which Jesus mentions the messiah Son of David is to deny the concept entirely. To the "[Pharisaic] scribes [who] say that the Messiah is the Son of David," Jesus polemically replies that it cannot be because "David himself calls him Lord; so how can he be his son?" (Mark 12:35–37). The messianic idea that Jesus refers to is the Enochic belief in the Son of Man, a preexisting heavenly figure, whose name is "hidden" from the moment of creation to the time of the end, when he reveals himself as the Judge, and "comes in the glory of his Father with the holy angels" (Mark 8:38). With the coming of the Son of Man, the power of the "strong man" of this world is put to an end, for "one stronger than he" has come (Luke 11:22), one that has the power to tie him up and "plunder his property" (Mark 3:27). The "blasphemy" of which Jesus was guilty before the high priest was neither the messianic self-proclamation of a prisoner without power (such proclamation would have been a matter of pity or laughter) nor a statement of a fully divine identity (which is not implied in the question of the high priest nor in the answer of Jesus). Facing the question of his messiahship, which for all Jews involved a special filial relationship with the Father ("Are you the Messiah, the Son of the Blessed?"), Jesus claimed a superhuman, heavenly identity, "I am; and 'you will see the Son of Man seated at the right hand of the Power,' and 'coming with the clouds of heaven'" (Mark 14:61–62).

Conclusion

A fundamental divide separated the followers of Jesus from other Second Temple Jewish groups that shared similar eschatological expectations. Jesus's disciples believed that the messiah (the "bridegroom") had already come, while "John's disciples and the Pharisees" believed that the messiah was yet to come (Mark 2:18–20; Matt 9:14–15; Luke 5:33–35). However, it would be simplistic to say that the identity of the messiah was the only or main issue, as William D. Davies concluded.[13] Second Temple Jews had

13. William D. Davies, *Paul and Rabbinic Judaism: Some Rabbinic Elements in Pauline Theology* (London: SPCK, 1948); see also Brad H. Young, *Paul the Jewish Theologian: A Pharisee among Christians, Jews, and Gentiles* (Peabody, MA: Hendrickson, 1998).

different ideas about the eschatological messiah, and different messianic expectations were framed within different theological worldviews.

The claims of the early followers of Jesus included not only the belief that the messiah had already come but also and foremost the acceptance of why the messiah had come before the end and what he was expected to accomplish.

By the time the synoptic tradition was formed, the early followers of Jesus had developed a distinct view: Jesus did not come simply to reveal the messiah's name and identity and announce that the end was near. A prophet would have been sufficient to fulfill this task. From their viewpoint this was the mission accomplished by John the Baptist. But Jesus was greater than John the Baptist. They understood Jesus in apocalyptic terms. He was the Son of Man, the final judge and destroyer of evil at the end of time.

They did not claim that the first coming of Jesus meant the final destruction of evil forces. Jesus the Son of Man had power over the evil spirits but had not come to destroy them yet. When the unclean spirit cried out: "What have you to do with us, Jesus of Nazareth? Have you come to destroy us? I know who you are, the Holy One of God," Jesus rebuked him (Mark 1:23–25). This was not yet the time of the last judgment, when the Son of Man will deliver the sinners "into the eternal fire prepared for the devil and his angels" (Matt 25:41).

Why then did the Judge come before the end, before the last judgment that God appointed him to preside over? The early followers of Jesus had a clear answer. In the process of restoring God's kingdom, Jesus the messiah accomplished a well-defined mission. He came as "the Son of Man [who] has authority on earth to forgive sins" (Mark 2:10; Matt 9:6; Luke 5:24).

Chapter 5

The Eschatological Gift of Forgiveness

Forgiveness of Sins in the Enochic Tradition

Speaking of forgiveness of sins in the apocalyptic tradition, and in particular in its Enochic stream, may seem paradoxical. At the center of the Enochic "theology of complaint" is the apparently absolute rejection of God's forgiveness of sins. In the introduction to his commentary, Nickelsburg devotes only a brief paragraph to what he defines as "a minor issue in 1 Enoch" and attributes this lack of interest in the subject to "its black-and-white distinction between the righteous and the sinners."[1]

The issue has important ramifications for the study of the relations between the Jewish apocalyptic traditions and Christian origins. The absence of any reference to God's forgiveness is one of the major obstacles in establishing a close connection and continuity between the Enoch books and the writings of the early Jesus movement, in which the idea of forgiveness of sins takes center stage. What does the forgiving Jesus have to do with the unforgiving Enoch?

At first glance a reading of 1 Enoch seems to confirm Nickelsburg's conclusion. The message of repentance and forgiveness is significantly missing in 1 Enoch. Enoch was chosen by God not as a preacher of forgiveness but rather as a messenger of unforgiveness—to announce to the fallen angels that "there will be no forgiveness for them" (1 En. 12). A compassionate

1. George W. E. Nickelsburg, *1 Enoch 1*, Hermeneia (Minneapolis: Fortress, 2001), 54.

Enoch agreed to intercede on behalf of the fallen angels and "drew up a petition for them that they might find forgiveness, and read their petition in the presence of the Lord of Heaven" (13:4–5), only to be lectured by God. Enoch had to report back to the fallen angels that their petition "will not be accepted." The last word of God leaves no room for any hope of forgiveness: "Say to them: You have no peace" (16:4).

The message, loud and clear, that the angelic sin cannot be forgiven belongs to the generative idea of Enochic Judaism. If the angels had been forgiven, the entire Enochic system would have collapsed. This world is an evil world exactly because the angelic sin cannot be forgiven and the original goodness of the universe cannot be restored until a new creation is established at the end of time.

Later Enochic texts, both Dream Visions and the Epistle of Enoch, draw a clear distinction between the righteous and sinners and make no reference to forgiveness of sins. In the Animal Apocalypse there are white sheep who open their eyes, but no black sheep turns white. In the Epistle of Enoch the opposition between the righteous and sinners is turned into a social conflict between the rich and the poor, the oppressors and the oppressed, the haves and the have-nots.[2]

The introductory chapters of the book of Enoch also sharply divide humankind into two fields: "forgiveness of sins, and all mercy and peace and clemency" are promised to the righteous, resulting in "salvation," whereas "for all you sinners there will be no salvation, but upon you a curse will abide" (1 En. 5:6).

And yet, despite the consistency of the entire Enochic tradition on the rejection of forgiveness of sins for sinners, something changes substantially with the Parables of Enoch. At first the Book of Parables seems to reiterate in its language of revenge and judgment the same attitude of uncompromising opposition between the oppressed and the oppressors, the righteous and sinners, that we have seen in the previous Enoch books.

With language that is reminiscent of the Book of the Watchers, Parables states that in the last judgment the sinners will be punished, in par-

2. On the Epistle of Enoch in particular, see Loren T. Stuckenbruck, *1 Enoch 91–108*, CEJL (Berlin: de Gruyter, 2007).

ticular the "kings and the mighty," whose destiny will be similar to that of the fallen angels at the beginning of creation: "No one will seek mercy for them from the Lord of the Spirits" (1 En. 38:6). Their own deeds will condemn them: "And in those days Enoch received books of zeal and wrath, and books of disquiet and expulsion. And mercy shall not be accorded to them, said the Lord of Spirits" (39:2).

On the other hand, the righteous will be saved. The four archangels will intercede on their behalf, "uttering praises before the Lord of glory" (1 En. 40:3). Quite mysteriously the task of the fourth archangel is announced to be that of "fending off the satans and forbidding them to come before the Lord of Spirits to accuse them who dwell on the earth" (40:7–8). In the Book of the Watchers (1 En. 9–11) the four archangels (named Michael, Raphael, Gabriel, and Uriel) preside over the punishment of the fallen angels and the salvation of the righteous. Here in action is the same group: Michael, Raphael, and Gabriel, but the fourth is revealed to be "Phanuel, who is set over the repentance unto hope of those who inherit eternal life" (40:9). The text suggests that repentance will play a role in the last judgment. Some will be saved not because of their good deeds but because of their repentance and because the satans will be prevented from presenting their accusations before God. The satans mentioned here are neither the rebellious angels nor the evil spirits but the accuser angels who will act as prosecutors in the last judgment by reporting the evil deeds of individuals (cf. Zech 3:1–7). No further details are provided in chapter 40. But the fact that the Book of Parables felt compelled to replace Uriel (an angel of punishment) with Phanuel (an angel of repentance, never mentioned before in the tradition of Enoch) indicates that something has changed in the idea of judgment. It is no longer presented exclusively as a judgment of destruction of evil (and salvation for the righteous) but suggests some more nuanced merciful act toward the sinners.

The text of 1 Enoch 48 emphasizes the revelation of the messiah Son of Man in the last judgment. The reference is explicitly to Daniel 7, but contrary to the source text, the Son of Man is not the recipient of God's judgment but is now the Judge, sitting on the throne of God. The last judgment will be according to each one's deeds. The righteous will be saved in the name of God since they are filled with good works and "have hated and despised this world of unrighteousness" (1 En. 48:7). An opposite destiny awaits sinners, kings, and the mighty; they will not be saved "because of the works of their hands" (48:8).

A brief interlude (chap. 49) follows, in which the justice of God and the elect is praised. Then in chapters 50–51 the judgment is presented in its more universal dimension, as the days in which "the earth will give back what has been entrusted to it and Sheol will give back what it has received" (1 En. 51:1). As expected, it is repeated that the righteous will be rewarded and sinners punished according to their deeds. However, quite unexpectedly a third group (the "others") is here singled out besides the righteous and the sinners—they are "those who repent and abandon the works of their hands":

> And in those days a change shall take place for the holy and chosen, and the light of days will dwell upon them, and glory and honor will return to the holy. On the day of distress, evil will be stored up against the sinners. And the righteous will be victorious in the name of the Lord of Spirits: and He will cause the others to witness [this], so that they may repent and abandon the works of their hands. They will have no honor in the presence of the Lord of Spirits, yet through His name they will be saved, and the Lord of Spirits will have mercy on them, for great is His mercy. And He is righteous in His judgement, and in the presence of His glory unrighteousness will not stand: at His judgement the unrepentant will perish in His presence. "And hereafter I will have no mercy on them," says the Lord of Spirits. (1 En. 50:1–5)

In the context of the Enochic tradition, this passage is extremely important, because for the first time it introduces the idea that repentance at the time of the last judgment will cause God to forgive some sinners by mercy. The passage, however, has not received the attention it deserves and has been mistranslated and misinterpreted even in the most recent and comprehensive commentaries to the Book of Parables by Sabino Chialà (1997), Daniel Olson (2004), and George Nickelsburg (2012).[3]

3. Sabino Chialà, *Libro delle parabole di Enoc: testo e commento* (Brescia: Paideia,

With the majority of manuscripts and all previous translations, Chialà correctly translates verse 3 as "they will have no honor," in the sense that they will have no "merit" before God. In the commentary, however, Chialà understands the verse as referring to the "righteous": *they* (not the "others") are the subject of the sentence. Chialà interprets the verse as a general statement that God's judgment is based exclusively on God's mercy even for the righteous, who cannot claim any "honor" before God. But this contradicts what the Book of Parables had just said in chapter 48; the righteous have good works, whereas the sinners do not. Besides, here the author refers to the "others" (the ones who repent and abandon the works of their hands), as is proved by the fact that the following verses (4–5) continue the discussion about repentance, not "righteousness," to the extent that "the sinners" are now referred to as "the unrepentant."[4]

Olson is aware of the presence of some manuscripts in which the negative ("no honor") is omitted but recognizes that the salvation of the "others" is presented in the passage as an act of God's mercy. "Jesus's parable of the workers in the vineyard makes a similar point."[5] The "others" are therefore sinners. Olson concludes that the "others" must be gentiles. "This chapter presupposes a time of relief and prosperity for the righteous during which the Gentiles may repent and convert."[6] The text, however, does not mention gentiles, and the Enochic tradition never states that only the gentiles are sinners, whereas the Jews are all "righteous." The "others" are "sinners who repent" (Jews and gentiles alike) as opposed to the "righteous."

Nickelsburg also correctly identifies the "others" as a distinct group—an intermediate group between the righteous and the sinners—but rather understands them as a subgroup of "the righteous" who may not possess the same merits but will share the same destiny. "Given the references to the righteous and their oppressors in vv. 1–2b, 'the others' mentioned in

1997); Daniel C. Olson, *Enoch: A New Translation* (North Richland Hills, TX: BIBAL Press, 2004); George W. E. Nickelsburg and James C. VanderKam, *1 Enoch* 2, Hermeneia (Minneapolis: Fortress, 2012).

4. Chialà, *Libro delle parabole*, 224.

5. Olson, *Enoch*, 94.

6. Olson, *Enoch*, 94.

this action must be either the gentiles not included among the oppressors of the righteous or other Israelites not included among the righteous, the holy, and the chosen."[7] To reinforce his own interpretation Nickelsburg somewhat arbitrarily corrects the text, based on the testimony of only two manuscripts against most manuscripts (and previous translations like Charles, Olson, and Chialà), and suppresses the negative (translating the passage as "they will have honor" instead of "they will have no honor"). Like the righteous, the "others" will have "honor" before God and will be saved in God's name. But the "others" are not defined in the text by who they are but by what they do ("they repent and abandon the works of their hands"). Nickelsburg's interpretation that the "works of their hands" is a reference to idolatry is contradicted by the same phrase used in 48:8 to denote the sinners ("the strong who possess the land because of the works of their hands . . . will not be saved"). The "others" are not "good gentiles" or "not-so-bad Israelites"; like the sinners, they can claim no honor before God.

Chialà, Olson, and Nickelsburg all miss the revolutionary importance of this text, which envisions the emergence of a third group alongside "the righteous" and "the sinners" at the end of time. The righteous have "honor" (merit, good deeds) and are saved in the name of God, whereas "the sinners" have no honor (no good deeds) and are not saved in the name of God. The "others" are neither a subgroup of the righteous nor a less guilty group of sinners or gentiles. Rather, as the text explicitly states, they are a subgroup of the sinners who will repent and abandon the works of their hands. Like the sinners (and unlike the righteous), the "others" have no "honor" (no merit or good works) before God, but because of their repentance they will be justified and saved in the name of God, like the righteous (and unlike the unrepentant sinners).

In other words, the text does not merely explore the relation between God's mercy and God's justice in the last judgment, a theme that is broadly discussed in the early rabbinic movement. That no one (not even the righteous) is saved without some intervention of God's mercy is a shared as-

7. Nickelsburg and VanderKam, *1 Enoch 2*, 182.

sumption in the entire Jewish tradition. This text in 1 Enoch 50 raises the possibility that some sinners will be justified by God's mercy alone, apart from God's justice.

According to the Book of Parables, the righteous will be saved according to God's justice and mercy, and sinners will be condemned according to God's justice and mercy, but those who repent will be justified by God's mercy even though they should not be saved according to God's justice. Repentance makes God's mercy prevail over God's justice. No reference is made to the traditional means of atonement related to the temple or good works. The Book of Parables refers to the time of the manifestation of God and the messiah as a (short) time when sinners will be offered one last opportunity for repentance and justification. The time is limited: after the judgment absolutely no further chance of forgiveness will be offered to "the unrepentant." Those who do not repent will be lost forever.

We now finally understand the special function assigned to Phanuel in the last judgment. By preventing the satans from accusing the repentant sinners, the archangel of repentance will cause the "others" to be saved apart from God's justice. Through repentance some sinners will be forgiven by God's mercy. The "others" are justified sinners.

This interpretation of chapter 50 is consistent with the entire Book of Parables and allows us to better grasp the development of the text. Having affirmed that at the end repentance is granted to sinners who repent, the text must make it clear that nonetheless this possibility is not granted to everyone. It does not apply to the fallen angels (thus preserving the integrity of the Enochic system) and does not apply to the kings and the mighty.

In chapter 54 we are told that "the kings and the mighty . . . [are] the hosts of Azazel . . . and Michael, Gabriel, Raphael, and Phanuel shall take hold of them on that great day, and cast them on that day into the burning furnace, that the Lord of Spirits may take vengeance on them for their unrighteousness in becoming subject to Satan and leading astray those who dwell on the earth" (1 En. 54:1–6). The lack of support from the archangels (including Phanuel) confirms that no possibility of repentance will be granted to them.

The downfall of the kings and the mighty is made even more dramatic by the rhetorical development of the narrative, since their destiny contrasts starkly with that of the other sinners. In what Nickelsburg describes as a "pitiful spectacle of role reversal,"[8] at the time of judgment "the kings and the mighty and the exalted and those who rule the land will fall on their faces in his presence; and they will worship and set their hope on that Son of Man, and they will supplicate and petition for mercy from him" (1 En. 62:9). Once again the language is reminiscent of the Book of Watchers. As the fallen angels did with Enoch, the kings and the mighty will petition the Son of Man for mercy. They hope that they also might take advantage of God's mercy. But this is not the case: "But the Lord of the Spirits will press them that they shall hastily go forth from His presence, And their faces shall be filled with shame, And the darkness grow deeper on their faces. And He will deliver them to the angels for punishment, to execute vengeance on them" (62:10–11).

Even in the hands of the angels of punishment, the kings and the mighty "will implore [God] to give them a little respite, that they might fall down and worship in the presence of the Lord of the Spirits, and that they might confess their sins in his presence" (1 En. 63:1). But again their request is rejected. Their eternal place will be with "the angels who descended to the earth, and revealed what was hidden to the children of men and seduced the children of men into committing sin" (64:1–2).

Forgiveness and the Unforgiving Messiah

The Book of Parables does not attribute any special power of forgiveness to the messiah, who remains the judge and destroyer of evil and is deaf to the plea of the kings and the mighty. God's mercy operates through the angel Phanuel; thanks to his intervention, sinners who repent (i.e., the "others") are acquitted by the judgment of the Son of Man.

Yet the text signals a radical turn in a tradition that had never paid attention to the problem of repentance or forgiveness of sins, except to exclude such a possibility. Repentance is now a central theme in the Book

8. Nickelsburg and VanderKam, *1 Enoch 2*, 266.

of Parables and should be a central concern for sinners in the imminence of the last judgment. With the exclusion of the fallen angels and the kings and the mighty, God is willing to justify by God's mercy those who repent.

The Book of Parables does not elaborate on these points, but if we read the Synoptics about the preaching of John the Baptist and Jesus, it is like reading a midrash of 1 Enoch 50. Regardless of the issue of whether or not this interpretation reflects, adjusts, or corrects what the historical John the Baptist and the historical Jesus really did or intended to do, from the viewpoint of the Synoptics the time of the end has come and God's messiah has been revealed in Jesus. The prophecy of 1 Enoch 50 no longer belongs to the future but has come true in the manifestation on earth of the Son of Man Jesus and his precursor John the Baptist. Their entire ministry was dedicated to the "others."

The Synoptic idea of the first coming of the messiah as the forgiver is a radical, yet logical and consequential, variant of the Enochic system, an answer to the Enochic problem.[9] The concept of the existence of a time of repentance immediately before the last judgment and the prophecy that, at that point, sinners will be divided into the repentant (the "others") and the unrepentant, is the necessary premise of the missions of John and Jesus, as narrated in the Synoptics.

The historical John the Baptist, who lived in the wilderness, had numerous disciples, and was executed by Herod Antipas, is certainly a complex figure with his emphasis on purity and morality, but the Synoptic interpretation of his preaching places him in the trajectory of thought opened by the Parables of Enoch as the precursor of the Son of Man Jesus. John came to announce (or should we now say to remind people?) that "those who repent and abandon the works of their hands" will be justified by God's mercy, even though they have "no honor" before God. The imminent coming of the last judgment, when the earth will be cleansed with fire, is an urgent call to repentance and forgiveness of sins for those who in this world have "no honor." The urgency of John's call is consistent with the

9. See Gabriele Boccaccini, "Forgiveness of Sins: An Enochic Problem, a Synoptic Answer," in *Enoch and the Synoptic Gospels: Reminiscences, Allusions, Intertextuality*, ed. Loren T. Stuckenbruck and Gabriele Boccaccini (Atlanta: SBL Press, 2016), 153–67.

Book of Parables' view that at the end only a small window will be open for repentance and there will be no time afterwards.

Facing the Judge and the fire of judgment means certain annihilation for sinners. The solution indicated by John the Baptist is also based on a central narrative in the Enochic tradition—the purifying value of water. The model was that offered by the flood, when the earth was immersed in order to limit the spread of evil. Be baptized with water; otherwise, you will be baptized with the fire of judgment by the Son of Man. This is the message of John the Baptist as understood by the Synoptics, an interpretation that does not contradict the Christian authors' interest in presenting it as a prophecy of Christian baptism (by the Holy Spirit). What John the Baptist expressed was a call based on the prophecy of the Book of Parables (chap. 50). At the end of time God will offer sinners one last chance. If a sinner sincerely repents and abandons the works of his/her hands, even though such a person has no honor before God, God's mercy will prevail on God's justice, and he/she will be justified in God's name. In the Book of Parables (contrary to what the Synoptics would claim about Jesus), the messiah has no part in the work of forgiveness and remains the judge and destroyer of evil.

Similar ideas are echoed in the Life of Adam and Eve—a text generally dated to the first century CE—where the sinner Adam does penance for forty days, immersed in the waters of the Jordan (and it is not by accident that John also baptized in the living water of the Jordan). The first man (and first sinner) is driven by a steadfast hope: "Maybe God will have mercy on me" (LAE 4:3). His plea to be allowed back into the garden of Eden will not be accepted, but at the time of his death his soul will not be handed over to the devil, as his crime deserved, but carried off to heaven; so God decided in God's mercy, despite the complaints of Satan.

The Forgiving Messiah: Jesus

In the synoptic interpretation, John the Baptist, as the precursor, could only announce the urgency of repentance and express hope in God's mercy.

But with Jesus, it was another matter: he was "the Son of Man [who] has authority on earth to forgive sins" (Mark 2:10; Matt 9:6; Luke 5:24). After his death Jesus left to his disciples the power of forgiveness through baptism "with the Holy Spirit" and will return "in the glory of the Father with the holy angels" (Mark 8:38) to perform the judgment with fire.

As in the case of John the Baptist, there are discussions of whether, how, or to what extent the theme of forgiveness of sins was part of the original teachings of Jesus,[10] but the issue here is not about the historical John the Baptist or Jesus but the preaching of the early Jesus movement. Whether or not the apocalyptic idea of forgiveness of sins goes back to Jesus himself and was indeed "the center of his entire ministry," as Chong-Hyon Sung concluded,[11] it certainly belongs to the interpretative tradition on Jesus since its inception.

Significantly, the idea of forgiveness is introduced not as a moral commandment but in an apocalyptic framework, similar to that of the Parables of Enoch and John the Baptist. In texts like the prayer of Jesus (Matt 6:9–13; Luke 11:2–4) hope is in the imminent coming of the kingdom of God ("your kingdom come"), and the major concern is the power of evil as a consequence of superhuman forces ("do not bring us to the time of trial but rescue us from the evil one"). The plea for forgiveness is central, and seems to require as a prerequisite corresponding behavior toward sinners ("forgive us our debts, as we also have forgiven our debtors"). Still, forgiveness is here the prerogative of the heavenly Father, and no power of forgiveness is given to the Son of Man. As in the Book of Parables or in the preaching of John the Baptist, the expectation is that of eschatological forgiveness at the last judgment, when "the merciful . . . will receive mercy" (Matt 5:7). Commenting on the prayer of Jesus, Matthew makes the connection explicit: "For if you forgive others their trespasses, your heavenly Father will also forgive

10. Tobias Hägerland, *Jesus and the Forgiveness of Sins* (Cambridge: Cambridge University Press, 2012).

11. Chong-Hyon Sung, *Vergebung der Sünden: Jesu Praxis der Sündenvergebung nach den Synoptikern und ihre Voraussetzungen im Alten Testament und frühen Judentum* (Tübingen: Mohr Siebeck, 1993), 283; see also Teodor Costin, *Il perdono di Dio nel vangelo di Matteo: uno studio esegetico-teologico* (Rome: Gregorian University Press, 2006).

you; but if you do not forgive others, neither will your Father forgive your trespasses" (Matt 6:14–15; cf. Mark 11:25). Luke is lapidary: "Forgive, and you will be forgiven" (Luke 6:37).

In the final redaction of the Synoptics, however, the Son of Man Jesus is not only a messenger of God's forgiveness but also the principal agent of forgiveness. He is introduced as a man of authority, somebody who could say to the paralytic, "Son, your sins are forgiven," without committing blasphemy, since "the Son of Man has authority on earth to forgive sins" (Mark 2:1–10; Matt 9:2–8; Luke 5:17–26).

Developing a traditional pattern that connects God's healing and forgiveness ("Bless the Lord . . . who forgives all your iniquity, who heals all your diseases," Ps 103:2–3), Mark sees Jesus's power of healing as a manifestation of God's forgiveness: "Those who are well have no need of a physician, but those who are sick; I have come to call not the righteous but sinners" (Mark 2:17).

Matthew and Luke basically repeat Mark's message on these issues (Matt 9:12–13; Luke 5:31–32), with some significant additions. In the Matthean infancy narrative, forgiveness is what the angel indicates to Joseph as the specific mission of Jesus, reflected in his name: "You are to name him Jesus, for he will save his people from their sins" (Matt 1:21). Luke adds the episode of the sinful woman who in the Pharisee's house anointed the feet of Jesus (Luke 7:36–50). This episode is likely a secondary transformation of the narrative of the anointing of Jesus at Bethany (Mark 14:3–9), but that does not reduce the importance of the story. Whatever reason Luke may have had to censor the anointing at Bethany, he could have simply suppressed the narrative. Instead he transformed it into a new episode, which combines elements from the healing of the paralytic (i.e., the questioning by the Pharisees and the explicit declaration of authority by Jesus) with elements from the calling of the tax collector (Mark 2:13–17; Matt 9:9–13; Luke 5:27–32), where in a similar context of a banquet the recipient of the gift of forgiveness is not symbolically a sick person but explicitly a sinner. Rhetorically, the centrality of the idea of forgiveness of sins is confirmed by the creation of an episode in which Jesus himself reiterates Luke's own belief that the messiah had "authority" to say, "Your sins are forgiven" (Luke 7:48).

With the advent of the Son of Man, the power of the "strong man" of this world has come to an end, since "someone stronger than he" has arrived (Luke 11:22), one who has the power to tie him up and "plunder his property" (Mark 3:27). In this, according to the Synoptics, lies the superiority of Jesus over John. The baptism of John was a call to the sinners to become the "others" through repentance. At the end only the unrepentant will be damned. But John could only express a hope, based on the prophecy of Enoch and the belief that God is good and merciful and cannot remain insensitive to the cry and anguish of sinners who, like Adam in the Life of Adam and Eve, plead with God in repentance and faith. According to his followers, Jesus offered a more concrete perspective as the promise of forgiveness comes from the Son of Man himself. After all, who can have more authority to forgive than the one whom God has delegated as the eschatological judge?

Sent to the Many

Reading the Synoptics in light of the Book of Parables of Enoch sheds light on some parables that the Christian tradition attributed to Jesus. The parable of the lost sheep (Matt 18:10–14; Luke 15:1–7) defines the relationship between God and the "others." Luke's parable of the prodigal son (15:11–32) reiterates the theme but also adds a teaching about the relationship between the righteous and the "others," between those who have honor and will be saved because they have never abandoned the house of the Father and those who have no honor and yet are justified as well since they repented and abandoned the works of their hands. The examples could be numerous, but I agree with Olson that no parable is more enlightening than the one narrated by Matthew on the workers in the vineyard (Matt 20:1–16). The householder who pays the same salary for different "measures" of work gives the full reward (salvation) to the righteous and to the "others," just as chapter 50 of the Book of Parables claims God will do in the last judgment. God's mercy ("Am I not allowed to do what I choose with what belongs to me? Or do you begrudge my generosity?," Matt 20:15) prevails over God's justice, or, as the Letter of James will say, "mercy triumphs over the judgment" (Jas 2:13).

The rabbis freely discuss the relation between the two *middot*, God's measures of justice and mercy, providing flexible answers to the issue. Mishnah Sotah (1:7–9) sticks to the principle "with what measure a man metes it shall be measured to him again" and affirms that "with the same measure" God gives justice when punishing evil deeds and mercy when rewarding good deeds. On the contrary, the parallel text in Tosefta Sotah (3:1–4:19) claims that "the measure of mercy is five hundred times greater than the measure of justice." But the two divine attributes are never opposed as in the Book of Parables and in the early Christian tradition; on the contrary, their necessarily complementary nature is emphasized. Not accidentally, the rabbinic version of the parables will end with different words in which God's mercy is praised, but God's justice is not denied: "This one did more work in two hours than the rest of you did working all day long" (y. Ber. 2:8).

Reading the Synoptics in light of the Book of Parables of Enoch also allows us to clarify a recurring problem, a crux in Christian theology: whether Jesus came (and died) for many or for all. Because the idea of "limited atonement" sounds like an arbitrary restriction of the boundaries of salvation, most Christians today would prefer to say that Jesus came for "all."

But there is no evidence in the Synoptics of a universal mission of the messiah Jesus to every person. The point is not that some people are excluded or that there is a privileged group of predestined or of chosen among the chosen. The point is that as the apocalyptic forgiver, Jesus was not sent to the righteous (who will be saved in the judgment according to their deeds) but to sinners, so that they might repent and be justified.

That in the last judgment there will be "many" sinners in comparison to a "few" righteous seems to be a commonplace in apocalyptic circles. When in the Testament of Abraham the gates of judgment are shown to the patriarch, he is told that there are two gates: "One broad on the broad way, and the other narrow on the narrow way. . . . The broad gate is that of sinners, which leads to destruction and eternal punishment . . . for they are many that are lost, and they are few that are saved" (Test. Ab. 11).

The same imagery is used in the Gospel of Matthew: "Enter through the narrow gate; for the gate is wide and the road is easy that leads to destruction, and there are many who take it. For the gate is narrow and the road is hard that leads to life, and there are few who find it" (Matt 7:13–14). That the problem is that of salvation is made even more explicit in Luke: "'Lord, will only a few be saved?' He said to them, 'Strive to enter through the narrow door; for many, I tell you, will try to enter and will not be able'" (Luke 13:23–24).

In no texts in the Synoptics is there any evidence that all people will be damned unless they are justified, because they are incapable of doing good. The fact that the messiah concentrated his efforts on sinners, the "lost sheep" (Matt 10:6; 15:24), does not mean that only those who received forgiveness will be saved and the ones not included in the "many" will be damned. The opposite is true. The few—the righteous—will be saved and do not need the gift of forgiveness provided by the Son of Man. The mission of Jesus was explicitly compared to that of a "physician" sent to heal the sick. The righteous do not need a physician; repentance is for sinners only: "Those who are well have no need of a physician, but those who are sick; I have come to call not the righteous but sinners to repentance" (Luke 5:31–32; cf. Matt 9:12–13; Mark 2:17)—sinners, the many, not the few.

Who Is Excluded?

Apparently, there are no limits to God's forgiveness—"People will be forgiven for their sins and whatever blasphemies they utter" (Mark 3:28). And yet, like the Parables of Enoch, the Synoptics claim that there are exceptions to the universality of the gift of justification. There are no comforting words of forgiveness addressed to the "evil spirits," who are aware that the time of their destruction is approaching (Mark 1:24). The rich and the mighty also cannot be forgiven, unless they cease to be rich and share their goods. "How hard it will be for those who have wealth to enter the kingdom of God! . . . It is easier for a camel to go through the eye of a needle than for someone who is rich to enter the kingdom of God" (Mark 10:23–25; Matt 19:23–24; Luke 18:24–25). And as in the Book of Parables, once the judgment has been pronounced there is no forgiveness, either in the afterlife or in the world to come, as clarified by Luke in the parable of the rich man and Lazarus: "Between you and us [i.e., between Hades and Heaven] a great chasm has been fixed, so that those who might want to pass from here to you cannot do so, and no one can cross from there to us" (Luke 16:19–31).

There are, however, some important differences between the Synoptics and the Parables of Enoch. The messiah, who in the Book of Parables is the final judge and destroyer of evil in heaven, has now also become the principal agent of forgiveness on earth. Jesus has incorporated the mediatorial functions that in the Book of Parables were assigned to both the Son of Man and the archangel Phanuel (who hence never entered the Christian tradition and silently disappeared, his important contribution to the definition of the messianic identity of Jesus being completely doomed to oblivion). The double role (forgiver on earth and eschatological Judge in heaven) assigned to the Son of Man even adds a new exception, an additional sin that cannot be forgiven besides those of the rebellious angels and the kings and the mighty. "Blasphemy against the Holy Spirit" apparently has to do with the overt opposition of some to the mission of Jesus on earth: "'Whoever blasphemes against the Holy Spirit can never have forgiveness, but is guilty of an eternal sin'—for they had said, 'He has an unclean spirit'" (Mark 3:29–30). The words of the Parables of Enoch are now applied to Jesus: "At his judgement the unrepentant will perish in his presence. 'And hereafter I will have no mercy on them,' says the Lord of Spirits" (1 En. 50:4–5). The problem is not the attitude toward the Son of Man. The problem is the rejection of the divine gift of forgiveness. Unrepentant sinners will not be saved. "Whoever speaks a word against the Son of Man will be forgiven, but whoever speaks against the Holy Spirit will not be forgiven, either in this age or in the age to come" (Matt 12:32; cf. Luke 12:10).

The Synoptics also changed dramatically the times and the setting of divine forgiveness. In his first coming, Jesus becomes the protagonist of a prologue on earth that precedes and prepares the heavenly judgment of the messiah Son of Man. Forgiveness is still an eschatological gift, but the opportunity for repentance no longer coincides with the time of the last judgment. It is offered and granted to sinners (shortly) before it (through the mission of the Son of Man on earth), when the kingdom of God has not yet come.

The result is that while in the Book of Parables the experience of repentance is prompted by the self-evident reality of the end of time, in the Synoptics it occurs now in a much more uncertain setting and time, when people are still desperately longing for "a sign" (Mark 8:11–12; Matt 12:38–42; Luke 11:29–32). It requires the acceptance of a message that is not yet manifested, as well as the establishment of a personal relation with its quite unlikely messenger, an obscure teacher and miracle-worker from Nazareth, Galilee (Mark 6:1–6; Matt 13:53–58; Luke 4:16–30; cf. John 1:43–46). This is what the Synoptics express with the term *faith*. The forgiveness of sins offered to sinners requires the faith of the recipients in order to become effective, and thus faith emerges as an important prerequisite for receiving forgiveness.

As we have seen, in the synoptic tradition the healing power of Jesus mirrors his forgiving power. "Which is easier, to say to the paralytic, 'Your sins are forgiven,' or to say, 'Stand up and take your mat and walk'" (Mark 2:9). Jesus switches from one meaning to the other, making the two meanings interchangeable. Likewise, the same phrase "your faith has made you well" is used for both healing (Mark 5:34) and forgiveness (Luke 7:50). As healing was sometimes hampered by a lack of faith ("He did not do many deeds of power there, because of their unbelief," Matt 13:58), so forgiveness comes to a sinner only through faith: "When Jesus saw their faith, he said to the paralytic, 'Son, your sins are forgiven'" (Mark 2:5).

After the death of Jesus, his followers understood the announcement of forgiveness as their primary task before the final return (or second coming) of the Son of Man from the clouds of heaven. Not only did they claim that Jesus had "authority on earth to forgive sins" (Mark 2:10; Matt 9:6; Luke 5:24), but they also believed Jesus had invested them with the same authority. "I will give you the keys of the kingdom of heaven, and whatever you bind on earth will be bound in heaven, and whatever you loose on earth will be loosed in heaven" (Matt 16:19; 18:18), an authority that John 20:23

explicitly focuses on the power of forgiveness: "If you forgive the sins of any, they are forgiven them; if you retain the sins of any, they are retained." The authority of forgiveness, which was granted to the apostles, was given for a mission of forgiveness: "All authority in heaven and on earth has been given to me. Go therefore and make disciples of all nations, baptizing them in the name of the Father and of the Son and of the Holy Spirit" (Matt 28:18–19).

The same link between authority and mission exists in Luke: "Repentance and forgiveness of sins is to be proclaimed in his name to all nations, beginning from Jerusalem" (Luke 24:47). In Acts, forgiveness was from the very beginning the core of the early Christian mission, together with the announcement of the imminent judgment, and is singled out as the major accomplishment of the mission of the Christ: "God exalted him at his right hand as Leader and Savior that he might give repentance to Israel and forgiveness of sins" (Acts 5:31). Faith and repentance are prerequisites for receiving the gift of forgiveness in the name of Jesus. "He commanded us to preach to the people and to testify that he is the one ordained by God as judge of the living and the dead. All the prophets testify about him that everyone who believes in him receives forgiveness of sins through his name" (Acts 10:42–43). Baptism is the tool through which the authority of forgiveness granted by Jesus to the apostles is made manifest: "Repent, and be baptized every one of you in the name of Jesus Christ so that your sins may be forgiven" (Acts 2:38).

In the Parables of Enoch the decision to repent coincides with the judgment, and the act of divine justification becomes immediately effective, resulting in individual salvation. In the Synoptics justification now precedes the judgment: it becomes effective though baptism and forgiven sinners will have to live with it for the rest of their lives.

Life after Forgiveness

The possibility for people to be justified in life before the last judgment as well as the delay of the end (a time necessary to carry out the forgiving mission of the apostles) soon complicated the picture and opened the door for even more dramatic developments in the later Christian tradition. Although believed to be short (as the end was still announced to be imminent), an intermission now separates the time of forgiveness from the time of the last judgment. A new problem arose. Once a person was justified, what was he/she expected or required to do before the final judgment? The first followers of Jesus did not regard justification (forgiveness of sins through baptism) as insurance for eternal life but as the opportunity for a new beginning for those who were oppressed without hope by the power of evil. They did not think that the forgiveness of God made them exempt from judgment; on the contrary, they believed that the judgment will "begin with the household of God, it will begin with us" (1 Pet 4:17).

The problem is addressed directly in texts such as the parable of the unforgiving servant (Matt 18:21–35). Jesus is now answering a question that concerns not the prerequisites for justification but the responsibilities of those who have been forgiven: "Lord, if another member of the church sins against me, how often should I forgive?" (18:21). As an act of mercy, "out of pity for him, the lord of that slave released him and forgave him the debt" (18:27) and then left. But the forgiven servant was oblivious to the grace he had received. He was blessed with an act of justification, even though according to justice he deserved punishment. A new life was graciously given to him to live in. Nonetheless he sinned again by showing no mercy to his neighbors. When the king returned he judged the servant for what he did *after* being justified. It was a verdict of condemnation, *despite* the mercy he had received. The final sentence is a warning specifically addressed to all the sinners who have been justified by the forgiving Jesus. "So my heavenly Father will also do to every one of you, if you do not forgive your brother or sister from your heart" (18:35). Justification is not salvation. The forgiveness given by the Son of Man does not annul the reality of the judgment according to deeds.

The Gospel of Luke also talks of ungrateful servants:

> Be dressed for action and have your lamps lit; be like those who are waiting for their master to return from the wedding banquet, so that they may open the door for him as soon as he comes and knocks. Blessed are those slaves whom the master finds alert when he comes; truly I tell you, he will

> fasten his belt and have them sit down to eat, and he will come and serve them. If he comes during the middle of the night, or near dawn, and finds them so, blessed are those slaves.
>
> But know this: if the owner of the house had known at what hour the thief was coming, he would not have let his house be broken into. You also must be ready, for the Son of Man is coming at an unexpected hour. (Luke 12:35–40)

Peter's question, which rhetorically interrupts the narrative, emphasizes once more that this teaching is specifically addressed to the disciples of Jesus:

> Peter said, "Lord, are you telling this parable for us or for everyone?" And the Lord said, "Who then is the faithful and prudent manager whom his master will put in charge of his slaves, to give them their allowance of food at the proper time? Blessed is that slave whom his master will find at work when he arrives. Truly I tell you, he will put that one in charge of all his possessions. But if that slave says to himself, 'My master is delayed in coming,' and if he begins to beat the other slaves, men and women, and to eat and drink and get drunk, the master of that slave will come on a day when he does not expect him and at an hour that he does not know, and will cut him in pieces, and put him with the unfaithful. That slave who knew what his master wanted, but did not prepare himself or do what was wanted, will receive a severe beating. But the one who did not know and did what deserved a beating will receive a light beating. From everyone to whom much has been given, much will be required; and from the one to whom much has been entrusted, even more will be demanded." (Luke 12:41–48)

Justification is an important step toward salvation but is useless if those who have repented do not persevere in their righteousness: "You are the salt of the earth; but if salt has lost its taste, how can its saltiness be restored? It is no longer good for anything, but is thrown out and trampled under foot" (Matt 5:13).

Consistently, in its description of the last judgment, the Gospel of Matthew (25:31–46) presents only two groups, the righteous and sinners (the "sheep" and the "goats"), both judged by the Son of Man (the "shepherd") according to their deeds. There is no room for a third group as in the Parables of Enoch. This is not because repentance was not important. Rather, the first followers of Jesus considered themselves the third group, sinners justified by faith from their past sins and now put to the test like everyone else according to the deeds performed in their lives after forgiveness.

But there is a judgment scene in the Synoptics that is surprisingly similar to the Enochic judgment of chapter 50 of the Parables: the scene described by Luke at the crucifixion.[12] On Golgotha there are not three groups but three people who represent them—Jesus (the righteous), the good thief (the repentant, the "others"), and the bad thief (the unrepentant). Since they are all about to die, there is no life left but only a decision to make before dying. Here justification and salvation coincide. The two thieves are explicitly said to be guilty according to their deeds while Jesus is innocent ("we indeed have been condemned justly, for we are getting what we deserve for our deeds, but this man has done nothing wrong," Luke 23:41). As sinners, both thieves have "no honor" and deserve to be condemned by God's justice, but while one repents and will be saved ("today you will be with me in Paradise," 23:43), the other does not. Jesus is the righteous one according to God's justice, the good thief is the sinner justified by God's mercy, and the bad thief is the unrepentant condemned by God's justice. The memory and legacy of the tradition of the Parables of Enoch was still very much alive.

Conclusion

The early Jesus movement was a Jewish apocalyptic and messianic movement that claimed that the end of this evil world and the reestablishment

12. I would like to thank my colleague and friend Isaac Oliver, who first drew my attention to this passage.

of the kingdom of God were imminent. In line with the tradition of the Parables of Enoch, its followers understood the end as a time of judgment, as well as a time of repentance and forgiveness. They shared the view of the Parables of Enoch, that by God's justice the "few" righteous will be saved and the "many" sinners will be condemned. But God is merciful, and by God's mercy the sinners who repent will also be justified.

From this vantage point, immediately before the end, God had sent the messiah Son of Man as the forgiver so that repentant sinners also could enter the kingdom of God by having their sins forgiven through a merciful act of justification. The mission of the messiah was specifically addressed to the "many" sinners, not to the "few" righteous who will be victorious in the last judgment according to their deeds. The messiah was searching for the "lost sheep" so that they could be justified by God's mercy through their repentance. Only the unrepentant will not enter the kingdom of God.

This is the message that Paul the apocalyptic Jew received when he joined the Jesus movement, the message he accepted by submitting to baptism, and the message he shared with the other members of the group. It was in continuity with these premises (which he never questioned) that he built his missionary activity. When many years later he became known as the "apostle to the gentiles," the substance of his mission would not change. He remained faithful to the apocalyptic call that according to Acts he had received from Jesus Christ himself: "I am sending you to open their eyes so that they may turn from darkness to light and from the power of Satan to God, so that they may receive forgiveness of sins and a place among those who are sanctified by faith in me" (Acts 26:17–18).

Chapter 6

The Divine Christology of Paul the Jew

Low and High Christology

Ever since scholars like Adolf von Harnack, Charles A. Briggs, and Wilhelm Bousset began presenting Christology not as the result of a flash of revelation but rather as a gradual process of growth and understanding,[1] Paul has been understood as a fundamental step in the transition from the *low* Christology of the origins to the *high* Christology of the church fathers, or from the *human* messiah of Judaism to the *divine* messiah of Christianity. By retrojecting into the past the current dichotomy between Judaism and Christianity, the concept of a divine messiah was seen as a distinctive Christian idea, totally incompatible with Judaism, generated by the external and pervasive influence of Hellenistic categories. It is the process that Maurice Casey so effectively summarized in the title of his 1991 monograph, *From Jewish Prophet to Gentile God.*[2]

The contemporary emphasis on the diversity of Second Temple Judaism and the Jewishness of the early Jesus movement has radically changed

1. Adolf von Harnack, *Lehrbuch der Dogmengeschichte*, 3 vols. (Freiburg i.B.: Mohr Siebeck, 1886–90); Charles A. Briggs, *The Incarnation of the Lord: A Series of Sermons Tracing the Unfolding of the Doctrine of the Incarnation in the New Testament* (New York: Charles Scribner's Sons, 1902); Wilhelm Bousset, *Kyrios Khristos: Geschichte des Christusglaubens von der Anfängen des Christentums bis Irenaeus* (Göttingen: Vandenhoeck & Ruprecht, 1913).

2. Maurice Casey, *From Jewish Prophet to Gentile God: The Origins and Development of New Testament Christology* (Cambridge: James Clarke, 1991).

and complicated the picture. Scholars like Adela Yarbro Collins and John Collins have shown that the idea of the divinity of the messiah has strong roots in the royal ideology that the ancient Hebrews shared with the other peoples of the region, who all regarded the king as the (adopted) "son of God."[3] Daniel Boyarin has concluded that the notion of a divine messiah was not foreign to ancient Judaism. On the contrary, it was so widespread in the Second Temple period that the rabbis had no little struggle to remove it from their own tradition. In particular, the association of Jesus with the heavenly Son of Man situates the "Jewish" divinity of Jesus at a very early stage in the development of his movement.[4]

However, such a widespread recognition that Jesus was regarded as divine at such an early stage has complicated, rather than solved, the issue, since for ancient Jews "being divine" and "being God" were not identical concepts.

What we now mean by *divine* was not what ancient people meant. In particular, in the Greco-Roman world, "being divine" was far from being an exclusive attribute of the gods. It was foremost a matter of power, and there were many degrees of the divine, from exalted humans to the supreme gods. Bart Ehrman has spoken of a "pyramid of power, grandeur, and deity"[5] made up of beings that are more than human and bear different degrees of divinity. Following the ancient pseudo-Platonic treatise *Epinomis*, it would be more appropriate to think of a sort of truncated pyramid, since polytheism had several superior gods at the top, whom the Romans and the Greeks would have identified with the Olympic Gods.[6]

3. Adela Yarbro Collins and John J. Collins, *King and Messiah as Son of God: Divine, Human, and Angelic Messianic Figures in Biblical and Related Literature* (Grand Rapids: Eerdmans, 2008).

4. Daniel Boyarin, *The Jewish Gospels: The Story of the Jewish Christ* (New York: New Press, 2012).

5. Bart Ehrman, *How Jesus Became God: The Exaltation of a Jewish Preacher from Galilee* (New York: HarperOne, 2014), 40.

6. *Epinomis* identified five levels of divinity, topped by "Zeus, Hera and all the rest [of the Olympic Gods]" (*Epinomis* 984d–985d). Plato, *Epinomis*, trans. Walter R. M. Lamb (Cambridge: Harvard University Press, 1927). See also Walter Burkert, *Griechische Religion der archaischen und klassischen Epoche* (Stuttgart: Kohlhammer, 1977; ET: *Greek Religion: Archaic and Classic* [Cambridge, MA: Harvard University Press, 1985]).

Surprisingly, Jews did not differ substantially from their polytheistic neighbors in their understanding of the divine. Also for Jews the universe was populated by superhuman divine beings (angels), exalted humans and other manifestations of God. "Jews also believed that divinities could become human and humans could become divine."[7] The biggest difference was that the Jews conceived the truncated pyramid of polytheism as a perfect pyramid that had only one God at the top—their God—but still preserved the presence of numerous "less divine" beings. These less-divine, more-than-human beings could be still called *gods* by texts from the Second Temple period, not only because of the influence of the religious environment of their time but also because many passages in their own Scriptures had taken shape in a still-polytheistic context and legitimized the use of such vocabulary.[8] The result is that ancient Jewish sources apply the term *divine* to beings that in our understanding should not be considered as such. The scholarly attempt to normalize the language (through a distinction between *human*, *heavenly*, and *divine*, for example) may help, but it ultimately fails because of the discrepancy between contemporary and ancient usage of the concept and term of divinity.

If the attribution of divinity alone was not conclusive for making Jesus God, what should be considered the decisive step? Bart Ehrman and Larry Hurtado are the scholars who in recent years have most directly addressed this question. For Ehrman, the attempt to identify when and how Jesus "became God" is not the clear-cut divide that one would expect but a much subtler discourse about how and when Jesus became "more and more divine," until he climbed the entire monotheistic pyramid (almost) to share the top with the Father. Jesus, argues Ehrman, was first regarded as a human exalted to a divine status (like Enoch or Elijah before him), and then as a preexistent heavenly being who became human in Jesus and then returned to heaven in an even more exalted status.

7. Ehrman, *How Jesus Became God*, 45.

8. See, e.g., the frequent use of אֵלִים for subordinate divine beings in Psalms (29:1; 89:6) or in the Qumran *Hodayot* and the Songs of the Sabbath Sacrifice. References and discussion in Joel S. Burnett, "*ʾelōhîm*," *ThWQ* 1.178–90.

Answering the same question some years earlier, Larry Hurtado traced the origin of such a belief by asking when Jesus began to be worshiped by his followers.[9] In his view devotion to Jesus marked a unique development within Jewish monotheism, even before the emergence of an explicit theology of the equality of Jesus with the Father. Jesus "became God" in the very moment he was worshiped. It is certainly true that Jesus is the only person in Judaism of whom we have evidence that he was worshiped by his followers; nonetheless, the force of Hurtado's argument is somehow diminished by the fact that veneration was a common practice toward people of authority. Even within the Jewish monotheistic framework, different degrees of veneration could apply to divine beings other than, and inferior to, God. In the Life of Adam and Eve (13–16), the archangel Michael invites all angels to "worship" Adam as the "image of God," and the Satan's refusal resulted in his fall from heaven. The Parables of Enoch (1 En. 62:6, 9) suggests that at the end of time the Son of Man also will be worshiped, without implying his identity with God. In the end, both Hurtado and Ehrman fail to single out what in ancient Judaism set the only God clearly apart from all other divine beings, besides an undetermined "highest" degree of divinity or a "highest" level of veneration.

For some time, I have been advocating a different approach than Hurtado's and Ehrman's—an approach that focuses neither on the practice of devotion to Jesus nor on the question of the divinity of Jesus but rather on the discussion about his created or uncreated status, a crucial issue in first-century Judaism.[10]

When at the end of the treatise *On the Creation of the World* Philo summarizes the five major features of Jewish monotheism, he does not talk of divinity or veneration, but directly connects the unicity of God with

9. Larry Hurtado, *Lord Jesus Christ: Devotion to Jesus in Earliest Christianity* (Grand Rapids: Eerdmans, 2003).

10. Gabriele Boccaccini, "How Jesus Became Uncreated," in *Sibyls, Scriptures, and Scrolls: John Collins at Seventy*, ed. Joel Baden, Hindy Najman, and Eibert Tigchelaar, JSJSup 175 (Leiden: Brill, 2016), 185–209; Gabriele Boccaccini, "From Jewish Prophet to Jewish God: How John Made the Divine Jesus Uncreated," in *Reading the Gospel of John's Christology as Jewish Messianism*, ed. Benjamin E. Reynolds and Gabriele Boccaccini (Leiden: Brill, 2018), 335–57.

God's unique role as creator of all: "God has a being and existence, and he who so exists is really one, and he has created the world, and he has created it one . . . having made it like to himself in singleness; and he exercises a continual care for that which he has created" (*Op.* 170–72).

Ancient Jews saw God not only at the top of a hierarchical pyramid but also as belonging to a different dimension. What defined God was not so much that God was the most divine being and the worthiest of honor and veneration. The decisive factor was that God was the only creator of all. It was God's uncreated status that made God *God* and defined God's uniqueness. Therefore, the proper question about the development of early Christology is not how (the human) Jesus (was exalted and worshiped and) became God, but how (the human and then divine) Jesus became uncreated. In other words, Jews in the Second Temple period may not have conceived of a clear-cut divide between the divine and the non-divine, or between who might be worshiped and who might not. However, in their self-identity there was a sharp divide between the created and the uncreated. While being divine and being worshiped were a matter of power, and created beings could share some degrees of divinity and devotion, being the one God meant essentially to be uncreated.

The Complexity of Jewish Monotheism

Unfortunately, even when posited in these terms, the question is still quite complex, as the concept of Jewish monotheism in antiquity was also far more complicated than one would commonly imagine. Jews in the Second Temple period not only had no trouble with the one God and creator of all sharing divinity with some creatures (seen as inferior divine beings), but they also knew a great variety of manifestations of the one God. Their presence made their monotheism an extremely dynamic and inclusive concept.[11]

11. James F. McGrath, *The Only True God: Early Christian Monotheism in Its Jewish Context* (Urbana: University of Illinois Press, 2009).

Among such manifestations were Wisdom, the Spirit, and the Word. Even though they had been somehow begotten or generated by God, they also were uncreated, since they were not properly the product of God's creation.

These uncreated manifestations of God were an important component of ancient Jewish monotheism. They dwell in heaven but were sent and came into the world where they appear to have a sort of autonomous life from the Father. They connected God to creation and helped God communicate with his creatures. They ultimately made God the caring Father of the universe.

Such a dynamic view of monotheism contributed to form a quite complex religious worldview. On one hand, there were uncreated beings, including the solely uncreated God as well as God's begotten manifestations, often active as mediators in the world. On the other hand, there were created beings, including angels, spirits, and humans, all created by the one God. The attribute of divinity was applied not only to uncreated beings but also to those creatures who were given superhuman power by God—angels and exalted humans (first of all, the high priest and the messiah) who were believed to act as "mediators" between heaven and earth.

The contemporaneous presence of exalted divine creatures and uncreated divine manifestations of God occasionally generated tensions, especially when created beings were given a role and a degree of power (or divinity) in heaven that was even higher than that attributed to uncreated manifestations of God (who, acting on earth, paradoxically found themselves relegated to a lesser degree of divinity). This is the case of exalted human beings like Enoch or Elijah who now dwell in heaven, and in particular it is the case of the divine messiah Son of Man, who according to some apocalyptic traditions will sit on the throne of God in the last judgment, being given the second highest position in heaven, second only to God (1 En. 69:29). Such tension is at the origin of the "Two Powers in Heaven" controversy.[12]

12. Alan F. Segal, *Two Powers in Heaven: Early Rabbinic Reports about Christianity and Gnosticism* (Leiden: Brill, 1977).

And yet ancient Jews lived comfortably in a universe populated by so many divine beings (uncreated divine manifestations of the one God, as well as created divine beings). In such complexity they saw no challenge to their monotheism. The balance of the system was preserved by a clear and impassable boundary between the uncreated and the created, between God (and his begotten manifestations) and his creatures, with no exception, regardless of their divine status. The messiah Son of Man is created and remains such even when he sits on the throne of God. Nobody could belong to both dimensions, being at the same time created and uncreated. Philo does not even feel compelled to use the language of strict monotheism, almost carelessly calling the Word (*logos*) "the second god" (*QG* 2.26); his main concern is to clarify that the *logos* is not created, since the *logos* is the "archetypal model, the idea of ideas" conceived in the mind of the only Maker and architect of the world before the actual creation took place (*Op.* 19, 25).

The need to set a clear boundary between the created and the uncreated was the only problem that ancient Jews were passionate about, more so than arguing about an abstract definition of *divinity* or *devotion*. The endless discussions in Second Temple sapiential literature about whether the divine Wisdom was created or uncreated indicates that an inferior divine being could be viewed by some as created and by others as uncreated. It did not really matter if the attribute of divinity was applied to a created or an uncreated being; what really made a difference was whether a divine being was created or uncreated. In any case, it had to be one way or the other; nobody could be both created and uncreated.

The uncertainties about the status of the divine Wisdom derived from the fact that unlike the Spirit and the Word (both unambiguous manifestations of the God of Israel), her origin was not explicitly determined in the ancient tradition of Israel. Or better, as contemporary scholars recognize, since she came from polytheism as an independent goddess "acquired" by the God of Israel (see *Ahiqar* 6:13; Job 28; Prov 1–9), for a long time her existence in Judaism was more assumed than explained.[13]

13. Bernhard Lang, *Wisdom and the Book of Proverbs: An Israelite Goddess Redefined*

Second Temple Jews agreed that Wisdom was somehow used by God as a tool in creation but were divided about her origin. Sirach maintains that Wisdom shares "eternity" with God exclusively in the sense that she will be forever (Sir 1:1b; 24:9b). He is very careful to specify that "God only exists before the times and forever" (42:21) and Wisdom was "made" at the beginning of times as God's first creature (Sir 24:9; see also Prov 8:22–23 LXX). In other sources, Wisdom was seen as "begotten" by God (Wis 8:3; Philo, *Fug* 50) and as an eternal manifestation or effulgence of God (Wis 7:26). In both cases the authors seemed to be aware that a clear-cut decision had to be made since different features and a different language applied to a created or an uncreated being.

In sum, in the religious worldview of Second Temple Jews, no creature of God and no manifestation of God could be conceived of as at the same time created and uncreated. An exalted created being could be called divine or be worshiped, but only an uncreated being could be the one God or a manifestation of the one God. It may not be accidental then that ancient Jewish sources—which did not have any problem conceiving of the messiah as divine and even suggested that the Son of God might be seated on God's throne, bear the name of God, and be worshiped—never claimed that he was uncreated. As Yarbro Collins and Collins have pointed out, the term "son of God," commonly applied to the messiah in Second Temple Jewish literature and in the Synoptics, did not imply any notion of preexistence and incarnation.[14]

Therefore, the question of how and when Jesus became God does not coincide with the question of how and when Jesus began to be regarded as divine or how and when Jesus began to be venerated. Beings other than God could be divine, and divine beings other that God could be venerated. And there are strong indications that Jesus was indeed regarded as divine and that he was venerated at a very early stage of the growth of his movement. The correct question is how and when the divine Jesus began to be regarded as uncreated. Only at this point could it be said that Jesus was given the same features as the only God.

(New York: Pilgrim, 1986); Silvia Schroer, *Wisdom Has Built Her House: Studies on the Figure of Sophia in the Bible* (Collegeville, MN: Liturgical Press, 2000).

14. Yarbro Collins and Collins, *King and Messiah*, 209.

The Christology of Paul

The absence of any explicit references to the full divinity of the messiah in the earliest strata of Christian literature does not automatically link the first followers of Jesus to a low Christology or to the tradition of the human messiah, Son of David. Indeed, there never was in Christianity something like a low Christology centered on the view of Jesus as a human messiah. Since its earliest beginnings, the Jesus movement found cohesion in the belief of Jesus as the Son of Man, an exalted heavenly, divine messiah, the forgiver on earth and the would-be eschatological Judge. However, while exalting Jesus as a divine being and venerating him accordingly, the first followers of Jesus never considered the hypothesis that their messiah could be uncreated. This possibility was simply not part of the Jewish messianic debate of the time.

Paul was no exception. His Christology does not radically depart from the Enochic (and Synoptic) pattern.[15] Paul also was very careful never to attribute to the *kyrios* (Lord) Jesus the title of *theos* (God), which was unique to the Father. "Indeed, even though there may be so-called gods in heaven or on earth—as in fact there are many gods [*theoi*] and many lords [*kyrioi*]—yet for us there is only one God [*theos*], the Father, from whom are all things and for whom we exist, and one Lord [*kyrios*], Jesus Christ, through whom are all things and through whom we exist" (1 Cor 8:5–6). And in fact the basic distinction between the Father and the Son was not a matter of divinity; both were reckoned by Paul among the (more or less) divine beings. The Father is the only God (*theos*) not simply because he is more divine but because he is the uncreated Maker of All, while the (less divine) Son (*kyrios*) is the instrument the Father used to create the universe.

Paul knows a tradition that claimed Jesus "was descended from David according to the flesh" (Rom 1:3), but he fully shares the belief of the early followers of Jesus who attributed to their messiah not only messianic features but also a much higher degree of divinity, corresponding to his

15. James A. Waddell, *The Messiah: A Comparative Study of the Enochic Son of Man and the Pauline Kyrios* (London: T&T Clark, 2011).

heavenly nature and salvific functions. Like the synoptic Son of Man, the Pauline Son-*kyrios* belongs to the heavenly sphere but is separated from and subordinate to the Father-*theos*. After completing his mission of forgiveness through his self-sacrifice, "the son himself will be subjected to the one who put all things in subjection under him, so that God may be all in all" (1 Cor 15:28). If Paul does not use the term Son of Man (even in contexts such as 1 Thess 4:16–17, where the allusion to Dan 7 would have made it obvious), it is because the title would have interfered with the parallelism he establishes between Adam and the new Adam, by suggesting the subordination of Jesus ben Adam to the first Adam. Therefore, to preserve the parallel, "son of God" is used. As the obedient son, Christ is compared to the disobedient son, Adam, whose nature and dignity he shares as the other "son of God" (see Luke 3:38). Both were created in the image and likeness of God, each taking upon himself the "form" of God. Adam and Jesus, however, are separated by a different fate—that is, one of guilt and transgression in the case of Adam and the other of obedience and glory in the case of the new Adam. The lowering (*kenōsis*) of Adam is a punishment caused by his disobedience, while in Jesus the lowering (*kenōsis*) is a voluntary choice for accomplishing his mission of forgiveness and is followed by his elevation and glorification (Phil 2:5–11) to a divine status that is higher than he was before. The veneration of Jesus is evidence of Jesus's divine status, not of his uncreated status; it is the veneration due to the Son of Man at the time his name is manifested.

As Yarbro Collins and Collins correctly point out, the prose hymn in Philippians "clearly speaks about the preexistence of Jesus . . . [but] does not imply that Jesus was God or equal to God before his birth as a human being."[16] In Ehrman's words, "Paul understood Christ to be an angel who became a human."[17] Ehrman's interpretation of the Philippian hymn as an early example of "incarnation christology," however, is misleading, and his rejection of the parallelism with Adam is unnecessary. Philippians' description of

16. Yarbro Collins and Collins, *King and Messiah*, 147.

17. Ehrman, *How Jesus Became God*, 252. Already in 1941 Martin Werner suggested that the earliest Christian speculations on the divinity of the Son should be read in light of Jewish angelology; see his *Die Entstehung des christlichen Dogmas* (Bern: Haupt, 1941).

the lowering of the divine Son who became human as an act of obedience and was then exalted to a higher degree of divinity parallels the story of the divine Adam, the other son of God, who also was created immortal like an angel but became human (i.e., mortal) as a punishment for his desire of acquiring a higher degree of divinity. Yes, Paul describes Jesus as "a preexistent divine being,"[18] but there is no incarnation in Paul; in no place does Paul speak of Jesus as the uncreated Wisdom or Word who became flesh. Yes, "Christ could be a divine being yet not be fully equal with God." Paul is very careful; he never refers to Christ as the *theos*, the only uncreated Maker of All.[19]

It took almost a century for members of the Jesus movement to come to the conclusion (or within a Christian theological perspective, to the realization) that Jesus the messiah has "become as much superior to angels as the name he has inherited is more excellent than theirs" (Heb 1:4). And it took the ingenuity of the Gospel of John to first introduce the possibility of an uncreated divine Christ and make this concept part of the theological debate of Second Temple Judaism. This goal was achieved by relying on speculations about the divine, uncreated *logos/sophia*, speculations that were not completely extraneous to Jewish messianism, since it was believed that the messiah would speak the word of God and would be the revealer of heavenly wisdom (Isa 11:1–5). In other words, Jesus became God only when the Gospel of John ultimately made him uncreated and the messiah was understood to be the uncreated *logos* who became flesh. It was not the transformation of a Jewish prophet into a pagan God, as Maurice Casey argued, but the transformation of a Jewish prophet and messianic claimant into the Jewish God, exploiting the rich variety of Jewish messianic models and the dynamic nature of Jewish monotheism.

But this is not Paul. At the center of Paul is the forgiving mission of the obedient, heavenly Son of God, not his equality with the Father as the incarnation of an uncreated divine manifestation. In his view of Jesus as the divine

18. Ehrman, *How Jesus Became God*, 266.

19. Although it is grammatically possible that Romans 9:5 refers to Jesus as *theos*, no other passage in Paul supports the claim. Paul always praises God the Father at the end in his doxologies: "May God who is over all things be blessed forever!" See the careful analysis of Gordon Fee, *Pauline Christology: An Exegetical-Theological Study* (Peabody, MA: Hendrickson, 2007), 272–77.

and created messiah, Paul was as fully monotheistic as the other Jews of his time, though not monotheistic as monotheism was radically redefined by later Christianity in their view of Jesus as the divine and uncreated messiah.

The Death of Jesus for "Forgiveness"

Besides the parallelism between Adam and the new Adam (Jesus), what ultimately distinguished Paul in the context of the earliest Jesus movement was his emphasis on the Son's accomplishment of his forgiving mission essentially through his death. The experience of the death of Jesus must have been a trauma for his disciples. The kingdom did not come as they expected ("We had hoped he was the one to redeem Israel," Luke 24:21). The disciples scattered in fear. And yet it was not the end of the movement.

The idea that the messiah could suffer and die was not foreign to the Jewish tradition, and the first followers of Jesus firmly believed that the events surrounding the passion and death of Jesus had been foretold by Scripture, despite their initial lack of understanding: "How foolish you are, and how slow of heart to believe all that the prophets have declared!" (Luke 24:25).

After his death, Jesus was vindicated by God, who raised him from the dead. Jesus is now in heaven where he is waiting for his final manifestation as the Judge. The speech of Stephen directly reconnects Jesus, exalted after his temporary *kenōsis* on earth, to the Son of Man of Daniel and the Parables of Enoch: "Filled with the Holy Spirit, [Stephen] gazed into heaven and saw the glory of God and Jesus standing at the right hand of God. 'Look,' he said, 'I see the heavens opened and the Son of Man standing at the right hand of God!'" (Acts 7:55–56). The resurrection was necessary so that Jesus could regain his status and fulfill what was believed to be his task as the messiah. Jesus "must remain in heaven until the time of universal restoration that God announced long ago through his holy prophets" (Acts 3:21). As Boyarin rightly pointed out, "The exaltation and resurrection experiences are a product of the narrative, not a cause of it."[20]

20. Boyarin, *The Jewish Gospels*, 160.

The explanation of why Jesus died was also a product of the narrative. As the central task of the messiah on earth was forgiveness of sins, it was natural that the first followers of Jesus began interpreting even his death as related to forgiveness of sins, as a necessary step in his mission.

That "Christ died for our sins in accordance with the scriptures" (1 Cor 15:3) is not an exclusively Pauline idea. It can be found in Matthew ("This is my blood of the covenant, which is poured out for many for the forgiveness of sins," Matt 26:28), in the Letter to the Hebrews ("Under the law almost everything is purified with blood, and without the shedding of blood there is no forgiveness," Heb 9:22), and in 1 Peter ("For Christ also suffered for sins once for all, the righteous for the unrighteous, in order to bring you to God," 1 Pet 3:18).

The letters of Paul offer the earliest evidence of the idea that the death of Jesus was indeed a sacrifice and Jesus was the sacrificial victim. "For our paschal lamb, Christ, has been sacrificed" (1 Cor 5:7). This idea would be repeated in 1 Peter ("You know that you were ransomed from the futile ways inherited from your ancestors, not with perishable things like silver or gold, but with the precious blood of Christ, like that of a lamb without defect or blemish," 1 Pet 1:18–19) and of course in the Gospel of John, which puts it in the mouth of John the Baptist ("Here is the lamb of God who takes away the sin of the world," John 1:29) and makes Jesus die the very same day and the very same way as the lambs sacrificed in the temple ("These things occurred so that the scripture might be fulfilled, 'None of his bones shall be broken,'" John 19:36). Consistently, in the epiphany of Revelation 5, the Son of Man who stands next to the throne of God would now be portrayed as the slaughtered Lamb whose blood has ransomed for God "saints from every tribe and language and people and nation" (Rev 5:9).

In Paul the sacrificial dimension of the mission of Christ is emphasized to the point that almost nothing remains of the ministry and teachings of Jesus besides his death on the cross. In the letters of Paul, Jesus is distinctively a person of few words, and none of these words is a word of forgiveness of sins. The death of the messiah is the only action that seems really to count.

Paul had not known the historical Jesus, but his repeated claim that the death of Jesus was the central mission of the messiah cannot be explained only in biographical terms, as if it resulted from Paul's ignorance of Jesus's teachings. Paul's emphasis on the death of Jesus highlights the graciousness of the event and the initiative of God. Jesus died for the ungodly, the sinners:

> For while we were still weak, at the right time Christ died for the ungodly. Indeed, rarely will anyone die for a righteous person—though perhaps for a good person someone might actually dare to die. But God proves his love for us in that while we still were sinners Christ died for us. Much more surely then, now that we have been justified by his blood, will we be saved through him from the wrath of God. For if while we were enemies, we were reconciled to God through the death of his Son, much more surely, having been reconciled, will we be saved by his life. But more than that, we even boast in God through our Lord Jesus Christ, through whom we have now received reconciliation. (Rom 5:6–11)

Such emphasis is an invitation to explore the particular circumstances that led Paul to define this and other distinctive elements in his theology, not as the beginning of his discourse but as the conclusion of a long journey that started in Jewish apocalypticism long before the teachings of Jesus and in the early Jesus movement long before Paul became the apostle to the gentiles. A reading of Paul not only "within Judaism" but, so to speak, "from within" Judaism results in understanding his system of thought as a variant and outgrowth of previous apocalyptic systems.

Conclusion

Paul was a Jew and always remained a Jew. He did not leave Judaism. He joined the Jewish messianic and apocalyptic movement of those who believed that Jesus was "the Son of Man [who] has authority on earth to forgive sins" (Mark 2:10; Matt 9:6; Luke 5:24) and after his death saw themselves as apostles, called to continue his mission. The Christology of Paul does not significantly depart from that of the Synoptics. Jesus is the final judge who came to earth to justify sinners who repent. Before being a mission toward gentiles, the new faith was for him a personal matter. He was baptized, and for him as for all other members (Jewish and gentile) of the Jesus movement, baptism meant the same thing: justification—that is, forgiveness of past sins in the imminence of the last judgment.

There are, however, two distinctive elements in Paul's Christology: the parallelism with Adam (Jesus is the obedient Son in comparison to the disobedient Son) and the emphasis on the sacrifice of the Christ (forgiveness is presented as a result of the death of the Christ, through his blood, with no references to his teaching and his word). These two elements suggest the eagerness of the apocalyptic Paul to directly connect the coming of the Christ to the protology of the origin of evil on the one hand, and to emphasize the graciousness of the event on the other. God is no longer passive. The mission of the Son is more than a last-minute relief to the plight of sinners who repent. It has deeper cosmic implications. It is God's definitive answer to the problem of evil, God's triumph over the forces of evil.

Chapter 7

Justified by Faith, Judged by Works

Justification by Faith as the Core of Pauline Theology

In the traditional Lutheran reading of Paul, justification by faith is the core of his theology and directly affects his understanding of God's last judgment. At the basis of the Lutheran concept of justification is the Augustinian idea that a person is totally incapable of doing anything that could determine or affect his/her salvation. Original sin has completely destroyed human freedom. On these foundations Luther built his doctrine of *sola gratia*. The law spells out what people should do, but because of the original sin it is impossible for anyone to keep the commandments. The law only provides the knowledge of sin and ultimately leads to damnation, while salvation can only be the result of a gracious gift from God. Even good deeds are the result of grace and cannot in any way be understood as requirements for salvation. "Sinners, incapable of doing good, can be justified only by God's grace, through faith in Jesus Christ."[1] The "superiority" of Christianity lies precisely in the fact that it is a religion based on *sola gratia* accepted by *sola fides*, while Judaism is an "inferior" religion of works that gives to its followers a false and arrogant illusion of self-justification. "Justification by faith" is equivalent to "salvation by faith."

The difficulty of finding parallels with the Pauline concept of justification by faith in ancient Jewish sources as well as in other first- or second-

1. Stephen Westerholm, *Justification Reconsidered: Rethinking a Pauline Theme* (Grand Rapids: Eerdmans, 2013), 49.

century Christian sources was explained by Christian scholars and theologians by emphasizing the uniqueness of Paul in relation to Judaism, "the Apostle's independence of thought and his complete break from Judaism."[2] Indeed, as observed by all contemporary interpreters, "Judaism lacked a doctrine of the 'essential sinfulness' of humankind."[3] On the other hand, Paul's struggle within the early Jesus movement to affirm the authentic "Christian" message against the Judaizers appeared to Thomas F. Torrance a sufficiently strong argument to explain the "silence" of later Christian sources; Paul's message was so much "advanced" for his age that it was largely "forgotten" in the post-Pauline tradition before being "rediscovered" by Augustine and Luther.[4] According to Philipp Vielhauer, the Acts of the Apostles offered the first example of normalization of Paul's revolutionary message, recasting the apostle as a Jewish Christian who was loyal to the law and stressed its validity for Jews.[5]

In recent decades a growing number of scholars have come to dismiss the "justification theory" as the imposition on Paul of a much later Christian paradigm. In Paul justification was not a universal concept but his answer to the specific problem of the inclusion of gentiles. Other scholars like Stephen Westerholm have struggled to reaffirm the traditional understanding, once purified of its most derogatory elements, as the only plausible interpretation of Paul and evidence of his uniqueness. "Paul's message of justification . . . does not address a need peculiar to Gentiles, but the need of all human beings . . . inasmuch as all are sinners."[6]

The discussion has reached a level of polarization that seems to prevent any dialogue. Either Augustine and Luther were totally right in their understanding of Paul or they were totally wrong. Each party seems to have some good arguments in their support. Westerholm certainly makes a strong

2. Henry St. John Thackeray, *The Relation of St. Paul to Contemporary Jewish Thought* (London: Macmillan, 1900), 80.

3. Westerholm, *Justification Reconsidered*, 34.

4. Thomas F. Torrance, *The Doctrine of Grace in the Apostolic Fathers* (Edinburgh and London: Oliver and Boyd, 1948).

5. Philipp Vielhauer, "Zum 'Paulinismus' der Apostelgeschichte," *EvT* 10 (1950–51): 1–15. ET: "On the 'Paulinism' of Acts," *Perkins School of Theology Journal* 17 (1963): 5–17.

6. Westerholm, *Justification Reconsidered*, 15.

point when he notices that "if Jews like Peter and Paul sought justification in Christ, then they, too, must have needed it."[7] On the other hand, the proponents of a reading of Paul within Judaism correctly point to the fact that Paul in no place claims that the torah is no longer valid or denies the validity of Judaism. "There is no evidence . . . that Paul's problem with the law was connected with the impossibility of keeping the law fully, or that the law was given in order to increase sin so that grace might abound more fully."[8]

Both parties have a weakness, which is not only the failure to listen to the other side but also the tendency to create a totally unique Paul who in order to remain Jewish is completely isolated from later Christianity, or in order to remain Christian is totally isolated from Judaism.

But what if we read Paul in light of the Parables of Enoch and in line with the synoptic tradition? What if we try to see him as a Second Temple apocalyptic Jew and a follower of the Jesus messianic group, as we have defined him in the previous chapters? The problems of the origin of evil, the freedom of human will, and the forgiveness of sins are undoubtedly at the center of Paul's thought. However, as we have seen, these were not Pauline problems; they were Second Temple Jewish problems.[9] The originality of Paul was not in the questions, but in the answers. The Enochic apocalyptic context and the emphasis on forgiveness of sins may allow us to reassess the problem of justification in Paul from a fresh perspective.

All Human Beings Are "under the Power of Sin"

In the Letter to the Romans, Paul wrote to the Jesus community of Rome: a community of people—Jews and non-Jews—who confessed Jesus as the messiah and had received baptism. Why did they do it? They did it for the

7. Westerholm, *Justification Reconsidered*, 15.

8. Daniel Boyarin, *A Radical Jew: Paul and the Politics of Identity* (Berkeley: University of California Press, 1994), 156.

9. Gabriele Boccaccini, "The Evilness of Human Nature in 1 Enoch, Jubilees, Paul, and 4 Ezra: A Second Temple Jewish Debate," in *4 Ezra and 2 Baruch: Reconstruction after the Fall*, ed. Matthias Henze and Gabriele Boccaccini (Leiden: Brill, 2013), 63–79.

same reason that all the first followers of Jesus (including Paul) had done it: because they were told that the end of time was imminent and that this was the time when God would grant forgiveness to sinners who repented. Paul knew that in Rome he could count on some important connections, first of all Priscilla and Aquila, who were with him in Corinth and Ephesus. Yet he addressed a community that he had not founded. He had to emphasize the distinctive elements of his gospel but did not need to repeat in detail the beliefs he shared with all the followers of Jesus. A few allusions were sufficient. This world is dominated by the devil, but the time of the end of his power is rapidly approaching. "The God of peace will shortly crush Satan under your feet" (Rom 16:20). Paul shared the common belief of the early Jesus movement that the time of judgment, or the time of God's wrath "against all ungodliness" (1:18), was imminent. This was also the time when the Lord Jesus had revealed himself as the agent of God's mercy for "everyone who has faith, to the Jew first and also to the Greek" (1:16).

First of all, Paul reminds his readers that according to God's plan, the moral life of the Jews is regulated by the Mosaic torah, while the moral life of the Gentiles is regulated by the natural law of the universe. "Gentiles, who do not possess the [Mosaic] law, do instinctively what the law requires . . . though not having the law, [they] are a law to themselves. They demonstrate that what the law requires is written on their hearts, to which their own conscience also bears witness" (Rom 2:15). Paul does not know the later Rabbinic concept of the preexistence of the Torah.[10] Since "there is no law . . . from Adam to Moses" (5:13-14), he could not refer to the natural law as the "seven laws of Noah" (or Noahide laws), as the rabbis would do beginning in the third century CE (Tosefta, *Avodah Zarah* 8[9]; Babylonian Talmud, *Sanhedrin* 56a-57a, *Avodah Zarah* 63a). Paul borrowed the idea of a universal unwritten law from Hellenistic Judaism and its emphasis on the creative order (or wisdom) as the primary means through which God's will is revealed ("since the creation of the world [God's] eternal power and divine nature, invisible though they are, have been understood and seen through the things he has made," Rom 1:20).[11]

10. Gabriele Boccaccini, "The Pre-Existence of the Torah: A Commonplace in Second Temple Judaism, or a Later Rabbinic Development?," *Henoch* 17 (1995): 329–50.

11. Gabriele Boccaccini, "Hellenistic Judaism: Myth or Reality?," in *Jewish Literatures*

Having affirmed that both Jews and gentiles have received from God a law that makes them accountable, Paul repeats the undisputed Second Temple belief that on the day of judgment, God "will repay according to each one's deeds" (Rom 2:6). Paul never questioned that if Jews and gentiles do "good deeds" (following the torah and their own conscience respectively), they will obtain salvation. Evildoers will be punished and the righteous will be saved with no distinction. "There will be anguish and distress for everyone who does evil, the Jews first and also the Greeks, but glory and honor and peace for everyone who does good, the Jew first and also the Greek. For God shows no partiality" (Rom 2:9–11).

It is the same idea that he reiterated in 2 Corinthians and would repeat again at the end of the letter to the Romans. "All of us must appear before the judgment seat of Christ, so that each may receive recompense for what has been done in the body, whether good or evil" (2 Cor 5:10). "We will all stand before the judgment seat of God . . . each of us will be accountable to God" (Rom 14:10-12). Nowhere in his letters does Paul indicate that he had an understanding of the last judgment other than that.

The idea of the existence of "righteous among the nations" was not foreign to Second Temple Judaism. According to Dream Visions, the world to come will see the restoration of the original unity of humankind with the gathering of the righteous from Israel and among the nations: "And all [the sheep] who had been destroyed and dispersed, along with all the beasts of the field and all the birds of the sky, gathered together in that house, and the Lord of the sheep rejoiced with great joy because they had all become good, and they had returned to his house" (1 En. 90:33).

The idea was also widespread in non-apocalyptic circles. Philo talks of "righteous among the nations," people, "whether among the Greeks or among the barbarians, who are practicers of wisdom, living in a blameless and irreproachable manner, determined not to do any injustice . . . who consider the whole world as their native city and all the devotees of wisdom as their fellow citizens" (*Spec.* 2.44–45). They might be "a small number" (*Spec.* 2.47),

and Cultures: Context and Intertext, ed. Anita Norich and Yaron Z. Eliav (Providence: Brown Judaic Studies, 2008), 55–76.

but they are around and will be judged according to their deeds. Rabbinic Judaism also remained open to such a possibility. For the rabbis, however, it was not the Mosaic Law that was the highest expression of the natural law; it was the natural law that was made after the preexistent Torah. The "seven laws of Noah" (or Noahide laws) replaced the natural law as the foundation of the salvation of the gentiles. In the twelfth century Maimonides would present this view as a normative belief: "Righteous Gentiles have a share in the world to come" (Maimonides, *Mishneh Torah*, Laws of Kings 8:11).

As one would expect from an apocalyptic Jew and a Jesus-follower, Paul's concern was not with the righteous but with sinners. First of all he reminds gentiles that they too are subject to judgment even though they have not received the Mosaic torah. The law "written on their hearts" (Rom 2:15) is sufficient to make them accountable for their sins. "They are without excuse; for though they knew God, they did not honor him as God or give thanks to him" (1:20–21).

On the other hand, Paul reminds his fellow Jews that having the Mosaic torah does not automatically include them all among the righteous: "For it is not the hearers of the law who are righteous in God's sight, but the doers of the law who will be justified" in the last judgment (2:13). Being a Jew is not a guarantee in itself, nor does it mean special treatment. "Circumcision indeed is of value if you obey the law; but if you break the law, your circumcision has become uncircumcision" (2:25). Paul does not deny that being a Jew has an "advantage," since "the Jews were entrusted with the oracles of God" (3:1–2), but this will not prevent God from applying God's justice against transgressors. Paul accepted the fact that the last judgment would be "according to each one's deeds" (2:6).

But there is a problem. As an apocalyptic Jew, Paul had a dramatic understanding of the power of evil. In his view, this is not only a gentile problem, it is a universal problem. This leads to Paul's central argument: "All, both Jews and Greeks, are under the power of sin" (Rom 3:9). To prove his point, Paul cites a series of biblical passages or, better, crafts a composite quotation made of different biblical verses (from Psalms to Isaiah) which show widespread evil (Rom 3:10–18): "All, both Jews and Greeks, are under the power of sin, as it is written: 'There is no one who is righteous, not even one; there is no one who has understanding, there is no one who seeks God'" (Rom 3:9–11).

This passage has traditionally been interpreted not as a simple recognition that all people commit sins but as a general statement asserting the human inability to do good. As a result, "the apostle thought along the same lines as Augustine, Luther and Calvin [that] . . . sinners, incapable of doing good, can be justified only by God's grace, through faith in Jesus Christ."[12]

In so doing, the Christian interpretation has reversed the order of the discourse. The quotation has become the center of Paul's argument, even though the emphasis in the text is not on the quotation (Rom 3:10–18) but on the statement that the quotation intends to prove (3:9). Paul's point is not that all people are sinners, as proved by the fact they are all under the power of sin, but that both Jews and gentiles alike are affected by evil ("under the power of sin"), as proved by the fact that everybody sins. The goal is to show that sin is a common experience of Jews and non-Jews and that no one can claim to be spared from evil.

The awareness that no person is without sin is common to the Hebrew Scriptures (Eccl 7:20: "Surely there is no one on earth so righteous as to do good without ever sinning") and to the teachings of Jesus, where it is at the foundation of a long series of *logia*, from "First take the log out of your own eye, and then you will see clearly to take the speck out of your neighbor's eye" (Luke 6:42) to "Let anyone among you who is without sin be the first to throw a stone" (John 8:7). The Gospel of Mark goes so far as to apply the same rule to Jesus himself: "Jesus said to him, 'Why do you call me good? No one is good but God alone'" (Mark 10:18). Every Second Temple Jew would have agreed with this notion. The problem was not human sinfulness but the implications and remedies for this situation.

Does the fact that all humans are "under the power of sin" mean that everybody is so sinful that no one will pass judgment? Following Jesus's commandment not to judge, his followers were more than happy to leave the answer to God, fearing to be measured with the same measure: "Do not judge, so that you may not be judged. For with the judgment you make

12. Westerholm, *Justification Reconsidered*, 48–49.

you will be judged, and the measure you give will be the measure you get" (Matt 7:1–2; cf. Luke 6:37–38). Paul also, although he tolerates no immorality within the community ("Drive out the wicked person from among you," 1 Cor 5:13), reminds the Corinthians that the final judgment belongs to God ("God will judge those outside," 1 Cor 5:13). Scholars have long noticed the existence of a certain tension in Paul between the "Christian" idea of justification by faith and the "Jewish" idea of judgment according to each one's deeds. If everyone is a sinner and is justified "not by the works of the law" but only "through faith in Jesus Christ" (Gal 2:16), what was the point of affirming just a few lines before that God in the last judgment "will repay according to each one's deeds" (Rom 2:6)?

We cannot simply dismiss the problem, concluding that Paul was inconsistent in his doctrine of evil, or that the statement about judgment "according to each one's deeds" should be taken as a meaningless Jewish remain superseded by the new Christian doctrine. Claiming that Paul's words about justification by faith apply only to gentiles whereas judgment according to each one's deeds refers to the Jews under the torah may seem an attractive solution, but Paul makes no distinction between Jews and gentiles about this matter.

E. P. Sanders offered the most successful model to harmonize the two ideas under the concept of "covenantal nomism," showing that there is no conflict or contradiction: both in Judaism and in Christianity salvation is by grace but requires "works" to "remain in." "The distinction between being judged on the basis of deeds and punished or rewarded at the judgment (or in this life), on the one hand, and being saved by God's gracious election, on the other, was the general view in Rabbinic literature. . . . Salvation by grace is not incompatible with punishment and reward for deeds."[13] Following Sanders, Kent L. Yinger reached the same conclusion: there is no conflict or contradiction as the judgment by deeds "will not so much determine as reveal one's character and status as righteous or wicked."[14] The assumption

13. E. P. Sanders, *Paul and Palestinian Judaism: A Comparison of Patterns of Religion* (London: SCM, 1977), 517.

14. Kent L. Yinger, *Paul, Judaism, and Judgment according to Deeds* (Cambridge: Cambridge University Press, 1999), 16.

remains that justification by faith and salvation by deeds both deal with the final verdict of righteousness for eternal life.

But in the understanding of apocalyptic Jews (such as the early followers of Jesus), the idea of covenantal nomism was complicated by their belief in the superhuman power of evil. Justification and salvation were not synonymous. The Enochians would not have denied that salvation is ultimately an act of grace, but their doctrine of cosmic evil implied in the Book of Parables the expectation of an additional gift of grace and forgiveness to sinners who repented. In light of these apocalyptic premises, the early followers of Jesus believed that this additional gift of justification by faith had already been offered, in the imminence of the end, to those who welcomed Jesus as the messiah. The last judgment will be according to each one's deeds, but Jesus was sent to justify the sinners as "the Son of Man [who] has authority on earth to forgive sins" (Mark 2:10; Matt 9:6; Luke 5:24).

Consistently, in language that echoes the Parables of Enoch and the synoptic tradition, Paul reminded his readers (both Jews and non-Jews) that the end of time is not only the time of God's vengeance but also the time when God's mercy invites sinners to repentance. "Do you not realize that God's kindness is meant to lead you to repentance?" (Rom 2:4). The sinners who repent will be forgiven, whereas the unrepentant, or those who persevere in their "hard and impenitent heart, . . . [store] up wrath for [themselves] on the day of wrath" (Rom 2:5).

From an apocalyptic perspective there is no contradiction between justification by faith and salvation by deeds. As in the Enochic literature, the problem is not the law but the power of evil. As an apocalyptic Jew and a Jesus-follower, Paul knows that evil is not only the consequence of human transgression but also is the result of a rebellion in heaven. This makes it difficult (though not impossible) to do good, since doing good is not simply a matter of human choice. The reality of cosmic evil, victimizing and oppressing people, impedes the human ability to choose what is good. Some apocalyptic Jews reacted by claiming that cosmic evil was only a gentile problem, since Jews were protected by the covenant. This was not Paul's position. He sided uncompromisingly with Dream Visions against Jubilees, supporting the view that cosmic evil affects all humans ("all, both Jews and Greeks, are under the power of sin," Rom 3:9), against the view that the Jews are protected from evil. The only advantage is that "through the law comes the knowledge of sin" (3:20).

The Gospel of Paul

In Paul, however, there is a special emphasis. In his view, Jesus was not simply the messenger and agent of God's forgiveness but also was God's answer to the spread of evil. The grace of God through Jesus has come to counterbalance the power of cosmic evil, restoring the relationship between God and humans—all humans, Jews and non-Jews alike: "There is no distinction, since all have sinned and fall short of the glory of God they are now justified by his grace as a gift, through the redemption that is in Christ Jesus, whom God put forward as a sacrifice of atonement by his blood, effective through faith" (Rom 3:22–25).

The gift of eschatological forgiveness is totally gracious. It is given "apart from works prescribed by the law" (as it does not depend on human obedience to the law), is offered indistinctively to Jews and gentiles as both are affected by evil, and is made effective through the same requirement, "faith in Christ": "[God] will justify the circumcised on the ground of faith and the uncircumcised through that same faith" (Rom 3:30). Paul immediately makes it clear that this is not a challenge to the law, but on the contrary confirms what the law itself states. "Do we then overthrow the law by this faith? By no means! On the contrary, we uphold the law" (3:31). This happens not only because the Scriptures affirm that God has the power to forgive sins "by faith" (as proved by the case of Abraham) but also because in Paul's view the death of Christ has confirmed the covenant and the law by restoring human freedom, which was lost as a consequence of Adam's sin.

The parallelism between Adam and Jesus, which is at the center of Paul's Christology, is also the foundation of Paul's concept of justification, which allows him to establish a link and parallelism also between the superhuman origin of evil and the gift of forgiveness through Christ.

In Genesis there is no devil; the serpent is an animal "more crafty than any other wild animal that the LORD God had made" (Gen 3:1). It may have acted as a tempter, and certainly sinned, but evil is attributed to Adam's free will. Both the serpent and Adam are punished. The earliest apocalyptic tradition also did not connect the sin of Adam with the devil. Evil spread as a consequence of a cosmic rebellion of angels, which took place "in the days of Yared" (1 En. 6:6) and therefore some generations after Adam. Over time things changed. In the Book of Parables of Enoch 69:6 the serpent "who led astray Eve" is now explicitly identified with "Gadreel," one of the fallen angels. And in the book of Revelation (12:9; 20:2) and even more explicitly in the Life of Adam and Eve, it is said that the ancient serpent was "the devil, or Satan" in disguise.

Nowhere does Paul explicitly link the sin of Adam to the temptation of the devil or of a demonic agent, but since he was a member of the Jesus movement, it is hard to imagine he thought otherwise. He believed in the superhuman origin of evil and believed in the presence of the devil. Paul knows that the conflict is essentially between God and the devil. The devil is "the god of this world" (2 Cor 4:4) and the time is approaching when "the God of peace will . . . crush Satan under your feet" (Rom 16:20), a prophecy that directly echoes the curse of the "ancient serpent" in Genesis 3:15 (the woman's offspring "will strike your head").

The conflict between God and Satan directly affects the two sons of God. While the disobedient son, Adam, sided with the devil, the obedient son, Jesus, sided with God against the devil ("What agreement does Christ have with Beliar?," 2 Cor 6:15). This allowed Paul to establish a convenient parallelism between evil and grace, or between the fall of Adam and the "free gift" of Jesus, and to give cosmic dimensions to the mission of the Christ. Jesus was not simply the messiah sent as the forgiver; rather, the grace of God through Jesus came to counterbalance the power of cosmic evil, restoring the relationship between God and humans: "Just as one man's trespass led to condemnation for all, so one man's act of righteousness leads to justification and life for all. For just as by the one man's disobedience the many were made sinners, so by the one man's obedience the many will be made righteous" (Rom 5:18–19).

Does this mean that all of Adam's descendants are evil? Not necessarily. Paul shifts rapidly from "all humans" to "the many." "All humans" (*pantes anthropoi*) have been led to condemnation under the power of sin because of the fall of Adam, but only "the many" (*hoi polloi*) were made "sinners." Just as not "all" but "many" are those "made righteous" by the gift of justification offered by Christ to all humans.

The irony is that Sanders (and other interpreters) noticed the shift of emphasis between "all" and "the many," but only in order to deny that Paul meant that "all humans will be saved."[15] The Adam/Jesus analogy implies a perfect parallelism between sin and grace as well as between the sinners and the righteous. Just as grace affects all but not all will be "righteous," the same is true for sin. It affects "all," but only "the many" are "sinners." All are under the power of sin but not all are sinners, exactly as everyone is now under the power of grace but not all will be saved.

In line with the whole apocalyptic tradition of Enoch, Paul never suggests that humans have lost their free will and are now completely incapable of doing good. He never denies the holiness and effectiveness of the Mosaic torah and the natural law, nor does he imply their failure. On the contrary, he reiterates the holiness and justice of the Mosaic torah and the Jewish covenant, which were given after the fall as remedies to limit the spread of evil. Thanks to Moses, the Jews received a full awareness of the fall (Rom 3:10) and the prophecies about the coming of the messiah. It is sin that must be blamed, not the torah:

> The law is holy, and the commandment is holy and just and good.
>
> Did what is good, then, bring death to me? By no means! It was sin, working death in me through what is good, in order that sin might be shown to be sin, and through the commandment might become sinful beyond measure.
>
> For we know that the law is spiritual; but I am of the flesh, sold into slavery under sin. I do not understand my own actions. For I do not do what I want, but I do the very thing I hate. Now if I do what I do not want,

15. Sanders, *Paul and Palestinian Judaism*, 473.

> I agree that the law is good. But in fact it is no longer I that do it, but sin that dwells within me. . . .
>
> For I delight in the law of God in my inmost self, but I see in my members another law at war with the law of my mind, making me captive to the law of sin that dwells in my members. Wretched man that I am! Who will rescue me from this body of death? (Rom 7:12–17, 22–24)

It is this situation of dominion of sin, not an intrinsic weakness of the "holy" torah, that leads Paul to do what the Book of Parables of Enoch had already done: that is, to seek hope not only for the "few" righteous in a heroic attachment to the law (according to God's justice) but also for the "many" sinners in an intervention of God's mercy, a gracious offer of forgiveness of sins "apart from the law" (and God's justice). "But now, apart from law, the righteousness of God has been disclosed, and is attested by the law and the prophets, the righteousness of God through faith in Jesus Christ for all who believe" (Rom 3:21–22).

Faith in Christ and the works of the law are not mutually exclusive paths to salvation. There is nothing wrong in Judaism as a religion construed as works of the law. The coming of Christ does not supersede but supplements the gift of the torah. The law was given under the power of sin to denounce the presence of evil so that the righteous could be saved and the unrighteous condemned: "All who rely on the works of the law are under a curse; for it is written, 'Cursed is everyone who does not observe and obey all the things written in the book of the law'" (Gal 3:10; cf. Deut 27:26). God is merciful and "does not have any pleasure in the death of the wicked." Sinners are welcome to change their lives; all their faults will be mercifully forgotten—"if the wicked turn away from all their sins that they have committed and keep all my statutes and do what is lawful and right . . . none of the transgressions that they have committed shall be remembered against them; for the righteousness that they have done they shall live" (Ezek 18:21–23). The law, however, condemns those who do not follow its rules. Forgiveness of sins for sinners who do not "keep all my statutes" and do not "do what is lawful and right" is a different matter and is something that the law cannot grant and should not be expected to: "No one is justified before God by the law" (Gal 3:11; cf. 2:16; Rom 3:20).

Now under the power of grace an additional gift of forgiveness is given, in the imminence of the end, to sinners who have faith in Christ. "Christ redeemed us from the curse of the law by becoming a curse for us" (Gal 3:13). Justification in Christ is an eschatological opportunity given even to those who are not righteous and have not had the strength to change their lives but are under the curse of the law. It is more than a merciful act; it is a gracious act, given "by [God's] grace as a gift, through the redemption that is in Christ Jesus, whom God put forward as a sacrifice of atonement by his blood" (Rom 3:24–25). Just as sin came "apart from the law" ("sin was indeed in the world before the law," Rom 5:13), God had to react to an extreme situation of distress and counterbalance the action of the devil with an extreme act of mercy "apart from the law": "For while we were still weak, at the right time Christ died for the ungodly. Indeed, rarely will anyone die for a righteous person—though perhaps for a good person someone might actually dare to die. But God proves his love for us in that while we still were sinners Christ died for us. Much more surely then, now that we have been justified by his blood, will we be saved through him from the wrath of God" (Rom 5:6–9).

As a consequence of Adam's sin, "death" spread throughout the world, whereas "life" is now spreading as a consequence of Jesus's obedience. "Since death came through a human being, the resurrection of the dead has also come through a human being; for as all die in Adam, so all will be made alive in Christ. . . . The first man, Adam, became a living being; the last Adam [Jesus] became a life-giving spirit" (1 Cor 15:21–22, 45).

Without the apocalyptic notion of the superhuman spread of evil, the entire Pauline doctrine would not make any sense, since the (positive) action of Jesus is shaped after the (negative) action of Adam. "Just as by one man's disobedience the many were made sinners, so by the one man's obedience the many will be made righteous" (Rom 5:19).

Since evil has disrupted the good order of the universe, grace is the antidote injected into the veins of the world to create antibodies that can fight the disease. The end has not yet come, but humans, here and now, are no longer left alone and without hope. The healthy (the righteous) no longer live in fear and the sick (sinners) in despair. The physician has come. "Where sin increased, grace abounded all the more, so that, just as sin exercised dominion in death, so grace might also exercise dominion through justification leading to eternal life through Jesus Christ our Lord" (Rom 5:20–21).

The grace of Christ has cosmic implications. It marks the reversal of the progressive decay caused by the power of evil that affected the entire universe. The whole creation longs "for the revealing of the children of God." It was "subjected to futility . . . groaning in labor pains until now," not through its own fault but as the result of the rebellion of demonic forces ("not of its own will but by the will of the one who subjected it"). The time has come when "the creation itself will be set free from its bondage to decay and will obtain the freedom of the glory of the children of God" (Rom 8:19–22).

The entire debate about justification and salvation in Paul is still too much affected by the framework of later Christian theology, which came to affirm the universal inability of humans to do good. But Paul was not a disciple of Augustine. As an apocalyptic Jew and a follower of Jesus, Paul claimed that forgiveness of sins was the major accomplishment of Jesus the messiah for Jews and gentiles alike in the cosmic battle that Jesus fought (and won) against demonic forces. Justification provides sinners (Jews and gentiles alike) an antidote, or at least a much-needed relief, to the overwhelming power of cosmic evil, a second chance given to hopeless people. They were "enemies," yet Christ died for them. Paraphrasing the language of the Parables of Enoch, those Jewish and gentile sinners who received baptism placed themselves among the "others" who were once sinners but now are repentent sinners, justified by God's mercy. They have "no honor" (no merit or good deeds) to claim, according to God's justice, but have received justification by the mercy of God.

The problem is not how, in the face of the imminent judgment, anyone (Jew or gentile) can find salvation. Nor is it how the gentiles can find salvation. Paul's question is: how can sinners find salvation? For them justification by faith (forgiveness of sins) is a second chance graciously offered in the imminence of the end. All the first followers of Jesus (including Paul) shared the belief that Jesus was the "physician" who came "to call not the righteous but sinners" (Mark 2:17; Matt 9:12–13; Luke 5:31–32). For Paul, sinners included Jews and gentiles alike, the lost sheep of the house of Israel as well as the lost sheep among the nations.

The gloomy "theology of complaint" of the early Enochic literature is now a distant memory. A radiant hope was born from its ashes. Paul is thrilled to be the herald of such a message of forgiveness. This ministry is even greater than that of Moses. The law that saves the righteous could only condemn sinners. Forgiveness in Christ has the power even to justify sinners: "For if there was glory in the ministry of condemnation, much more does the ministry of justification abound in glory!" (2 Cor 3:9).

Are the Justified Also Saved?

The members of the church are not righteous people but repentant sinners (Jews and gentiles alike) who have been made righteous, justified through their faith in Christ. What will happen to them in the last judgment?

Sanders (with Karl Donfried) noticed that, in Paul's words, people "have been" justified by faith but "will be" saved by works (Rom 5:9–10; 13:11; 1 Thess 5:8; 1 Cor 1:18).[16] From the vantage point of the members of the Jesus movement, justification by faith belongs to the past, whereas judgment according to each one's deeds belongs to the future. But Sanders interpreted this language as evidence of a universal process through which all humans (Jews and gentiles alike) are saved by grace (as they are included in the new covenant in Christ) and confirmed in the last judgment by good works demonstrating their will to "remain in": "Paul's principal view thus seems to be that Christians have been cleansed and established in the faith, and that they should remain so, so as to be found blameless on the day of the Lord. . . . Paul is aware that not everyone consistently remains in the cleansed state."[17]

16. Sanders, *Paul and Palestinian Judaism*, 516; Karl Donfried, "Justification and Last Judgment in Paul," *ZNW* 67 (1976): 90–110.

17. Sanders, *Paul and Palestinian Judaism*, 452.

The problem with this interpretation, as Chris VanLandingham noted, is that it links justification by faith "to the verdict of acquittal a believer will receive at the Last Judgment." Rather, justification by faith "describes what occurs at the beginning of one's Christian existence, not at the end. . . . [I]t describes the person forgiven of his or her sins and freed from the power of sin."[18] Obviously, for sinners, justification by faith is a path to salvation; according to Paul, "the gospel . . . is the power of God for salvation to everyone who has faith, to the Jew first and also to the Greek" (Rom 1:16). Justification by faith, however, is not salvation by faith. What Paul has in mind is not the destiny of all humankind but the destiny of sinners. For Paul, as for all the first followers of Jesus, what has already been received through baptism is forgiveness of past sins for sinners who have repented and accepted the authority of the Son of Man.

Paul is confident that all those who are "justified by faith" in Christ will join the righteous and will also be "saved" in the last judgment according to each one's deeds. "Much more surely then, now that we have been justified by his blood, will we be saved through him from the wrath of God" (Rom 5:9).

Paul's trust is first of all in God: "I give thanks to my God always for you because of the grace of God that has been given you in Christ Jesus. . . . He will also strengthen you to the end, so that you may be blameless on the day of our Lord Jesus Christ" (1 Cor 1:4, 8; cf. Phil 1:6). "May the God of peace himself sanctify you entirely; and may your spirit and soul and body be kept sound and blameless at the coming of our Lord Jesus Christ. The one who calls you is faithful, and he will do this" (1 Thess 5:23–24). "God is faithful, and he will not let you be tested beyond your strength" (1 Cor 10:13). But Paul's trust is also in those who have received the gift of forgiveness, in their ability to do good deeds and remain blameless, now that they are no longer under the power of sin.

Paul tells the Philippians that "my prayer [is] that your love may overflow more and more with knowledge and full insight . . . so that in the day

18. Chris VanLandingham, *Judgment & Justification in Early Judaism and the Apostle Paul* (Peabody, MA: Hendrickson, 2006), 17.

of Christ you may be pure and blameless, having produced the harvest of righteousness that comes through Jesus Christ for the glory and praise of God" (Phil 1:9–11). He invites them to "be blameless and innocent, children of God without blemish in the midst of a crooked and perverse generation, in which you shine like stars in the world. It is by your holding fast to the word of life that I can boast on the day of Christ that I did not run in vain or labor in vain" (Phil 2:15–16).

Not only have the past sins (plural) been forgiven, but the baptized have been "set free from sin" (singular, Rom 6:18, 22) in the present evil age. "The Lord Jesus Christ . . . gave himself for our sins to set us free from the present evil age," Paul assures the Galatians (Gal 1:3–4), and now they live "in Christ" and are assisted by the Spirit: "We have received not the spirit of the world, but the Spirit that is from God, so that we may understand the gifts bestowed on us by God" (1 Cor 2:12). Paul expected the believers to produce plenty of good works ("love, joy, peace, patience, kindness, generosity, faithfulness, gentleness, and self-control," Gal 5:22–23) and remain "blameless." After all, they have received so much, and the time until the end is so short, isn't it?

But once again, justification by faith does not amount to salvation at the last judgment. To be forgiven of their past sins and freed from the power of evil is, for sinners, an important step on the path to salvation, but it is not a guarantee of future salvation at the last judgment, where only deeds will be assessed. Justification is not sin insurance or a blank check ready to be filled at any time. Despite his (over)confidence in a happy outcome, Paul finds himself compelled to remind his readers and fellow Jesus-followers that the outcome has not yet been secured. "While we are at home in the body we are away from the Lord. . . . For all of us must appear before the judgment seat of Christ, so that each may receive recompense for what has been done in the body, whether good or evil" (2 Cor 5:6–10). In a way not unlike the parables of the unfaithful servant in the Gospels of Matthew and Luke, Paul warns the baptized that after receiving forgiveness of their past sins, their goal is now to be found "blameless on the day of our Lord Jesus Christ" (1 Cor 1:8). The mercy they have received does not annul the justice of God: "Note then the kindness and the severity of God: severity toward those who have fallen, but God's kindness toward you, provided you continue in his kindness; otherwise you also will be cut off" (Rom 11:22).

Being freed "by faith" from cosmic sin is an important step, but it is not sufficient: "For you were called to freedom, brothers and sisters; only do not use your freedom as an opportunity for self-indulgence, but through love become slaves to one another. For the whole law is summed up in a single commandment, 'You shall love your neighbor as yourself.' . . . Live by the Spirit, I say, and do not gratify the desires of the flesh. . . . I am warning you, as I warned you before: those who do such things will not inherit the kingdom of God" (Gal 5:13–21).

Having the Spirit is a blessing and a "guarantee" (2 Cor 5:5), but also an enormous responsibility: "Do you not know that you are God's temple and that God's spirit dwells in you? If anyone destroys God's temple, God will destroy that person. For God's temple is holy, and you are that temple" (1 Cor 3:16–17). "Examine yourselves to see whether you are living in the faith. Test yourselves" (2 Cor 13:5).

This is not a message limited to the sinners among the nations. The personal experience of Paul the Jew shows that justification by faith is offered to all sinners (Jews and gentiles alike) and the same judgment awaits all according to their deeds. Paul switches from "you" to "we": "All of us must appear before the judgment seat of Christ" (2 Cor 5:10); "we will all stand before the judgment seat of God . . . each of us will be accountable to God" (Rom 14:10–12). With the Philippians, Paul becomes even more personal, declaring that his individual situation is no different: "[I do not have] a righteousness of my own that comes from the law, but one that comes through faith in Christ, the righteousness from God based on faith" (Phil 3:9). This does not make Paul automatically saved:

> I want to know Christ and the power of his resurrection and the sharing of his sufferings by becoming like him in his death, if somehow I may attain the resurrection from the dead.
>
> Not that I have already obtained this or have already reached the goal; but I press on to make it my own, because Christ Jesus has made me his

> own. Brothers, I do not consider that I have made it my own; but this one thing I do: forgetting what lies behind and straining forward to what lies ahead, I press on toward the goal for the prize of the heavenly call of God in Christ Jesus. (Phil 3:10–14)

To the Corinthians Paul conceded that he could not even be sure of his own salvation: "It is required of stewards that they be found trustworthy. But with me it is a very small thing that I should be judged by you or by any human court. I do not even judge myself. I am not aware of anything against myself, but I am not thereby acquitted. It is the Lord who judges me. Therefore do not pronounce judgment before the time, before the Lord comes, who will bring to light the things now hidden in darkness and will disclose the purposes of the heart. Then each one will receive commendation from God" (1 Cor 4:2–5). The warnings are real (1 Cor 1:18; 1 Thess 3:13, 5:23; Phil 2:15; cf. Col 1:22); justified sinners can lose their status by failing to persevere in good works.[19]

When Paul speaks of justification by faith, he speaks of something different from the last judgment according to each one's deeds. Justification by faith is an unconditional gift of forgiveness offered to repentant sinners who have faith in Jesus. Salvation is the result of the final judgment in which all humans will be judged according to their own deeds. Chris VanLandingham was totally correct in the conclusions of his study on *Judgment & Justification in Early Judaism and the Apostle Paul*: "A person who has been 'made righteous' is forgiven of past sins (which then become a dead issue), cleansed from the guilt and impurity of sin, freed from the human propensity to sin, and then given the ability to obey. The Last Judgment will then determine whether a person, as an act of the will, has followed through with these benefits of Christ's death. If so, eternal life will be the reward; if not damnation."[20]

This is the reason why "love" is ultimately the most important virtue (1 Cor 13). Faith is important because it produced justification; hope means

19. Preston M. Sprinkle, *Paul & Judaism Revisited: A Study of Divine and Human Agency in Salvation* (Downers Grove, IL: IVP Academic, 2013), 204–7.

20. VanLandingham, *Judgment & Justification*, 335.

perseverance in the future; but love is the greatest because for everyone it is the foundation of the last judgment. "Faith, hope, and love abide, these three; and the greatest of these is love" (1 Cor 13:13).

Paul within the Early Christian Tradition

When understood in these terms, the Pauline discourse on justification by faith loses its suspicious uniqueness and awkwardness in relation to Second Temple Judaism. It is now perfectly in line with the prophecy of the Parables of Enoch as well as with the message of first- and second-century Jesus-followers, where the two concepts of justification by faith and judgment according to each one's deeds coexist harmoniously.[21] Paul's teaching at Antioch of Pisidia was the teaching of the whole church; the announcement of the eschatological forgiveness of sins was the primary mission of Jesus the messiah: "Let it be known to you therefore, my brothers, that through this man [Jesus] forgiveness of sins is proclaimed to you; by this Jesus everyone who believes is set free from all those sins from which you could not be freed by the law of Moses" (Acts 13:38–39).

In the writings of the early Jesus movement preserved in the New Testament and the Apostolic Fathers, justification by faith and judgment according to each one's deeds appear side by side. No one in the early Jesus movement ever questioned that the last judgment will be based on deeds: "The Son of Man is to come with his angels in the glory of his Father, and then he will repay everyone for what has been done" (Matt 16:27). The words of reward (or punishment) for having acknowledged (or denied) Jesus "before others" are addressed specifically to the disciples only (Matt 10:32-33; Luke 12:8-9). To outsiders the criterion is the love they have had (or not had) for their neighbors: "When the Son of Man comes in his glory, and all the angels with him, then he will sit on the

21. Brian J. Arnold's criticism of Torrance's thesis that the Pauline notion of "justification by faith" was abandoned in second-century Christianity is still based on the assumption that "justification by faith" and "judgment by works" are two mutually exclusive notions. See Brian J. Arnold, *Justification in the Second Century* (Minneapolis: Fortress, 2013).

throne of his glory. All the nations will be gathered before him, and he will separate people one from another as a shepherd separates the sheep from the goats. . . . Then the king will say to those at his right hand: '. . . Just as you did it to one of the least of these who are members of my family, you did it to me.' Then he will say to those at his left hand . . . 'Just as you did not do it to one of the least of these, you did not do it to me.' And these will go away into eternal punishment, but the righteous into eternal life" (Matt 25:31-46).

An analogous judgment scene is presented to John in the book of Revelation. "I saw a great white throne and the one who sat on it. . . . And I saw the dead, great and small, standing before the throne, and books were opened. Also another book was opened, the book of life. And the dead were judged according to their works, as recorded in the books. And the sea gave up the dead that were in it, Death and Hades gave up the dead that were in them, and all were judged according to what they had done . . . anyone whose name was not found written in the book of life was thrown into the lake of fire" (Rev 20:11-15). The end of Revelation is a word of warning uttered by the risen Christ himself, which directly echoes Matthew 16:27: "See, I am coming soon; my reward is with me, to repay according to everyone's work" (Rev 22:12).

The message is the same found in Paul's letters (Rom 2:5-16; 14:10-12; 2 Cor 5:10) and, as in Paul's letters, the reference to the final judgment according to each one's deeds is a warning against those believers who through baptism have received the gift of justification and the Spirit of God and yet do not remain blameless. Similar warnings are common in the literature of the early Jesus movement, as in the case of the first letter of Peter:

> If you are reviled for the name of Christ, you are blessed, because the spirit of glory, which is the Spirit of God, is resting on you. But let none of you suffer as a murderer, a thief, a criminal, or even as a mischief maker. . . . For the time has come for judgment to begin with the household of God. . . . It will begin with us. . . . [Continue] to do good. . . . Humble yourselves therefore under the mighty hand of God, so that he may exalt you in due time. . . . Discipline yourself, keep alert. . . . And after you have suffered

> for a little while, the God of all grace, who has called you to the eternal glory in Christ, will himself restore, support, strengthen, and establish you. (1 Pet 4:14–5:10)

The Letter to the Hebrews also contains strong words against those who "have spurned the Son of God." They might have avoided judgment for the sins they committed under the law of Moses, but an even harsher punishment is reserved for them for the sins they committed after the justification they received through the blood of Christ:

> For if we willfully persist in sin after having received the knowledge of the truth, there no longer remains a sacrifice for sins, but a fearful prospect of judgment, and a fury of fire that will consume the adversaries. Anyone who has violated the law of Moses dies without mercy "on the testimony of two or three witnesses." How much worse punishment do you think will be deserved by those who have spurned the Son of God, profaned the blood of the covenant by which they were sanctified, and outraged the Spirit of grace? For we know the one who said, "Vengeance is mine, I will repay." And again, "The Lord will judge his people." It is a fearful thing to fall into the hands of the living God. (Heb 10:26–31)

With words not unlike those used by Paul, 1 Clement reminds the members of the church that they have been graciously justified: "And we, too, being called by His will in Christ Jesus, are not justified by ourselves, nor by our own wisdom, or understanding, or godliness, or works which we have wrought in holiness of heart; but by that faith through which, from the beginning, Almighty God has justified all men; to whom be glory for ever and ever. Amen" (1 Clem. 32).[22] And then he admonishes them that in the end they will face in the last judgment a second and final justification, this time based on each one's deeds: "Let us clothe ourselves with concord and humility, ever exercising self-control, standing far off from all whis-

22. On the First Letter of Clement and the Shepherd of Hermas, see *The Apostolic Fathers*, edited and translated by Bart D. Ehrman, 2 vols. (Cambridge: Harvard University Press, 2003).

pering and evil-speaking, being justified by our works, and not our words" (1 Clem. 30).

The second letter of Peter does not hide its great contempt for the baptized who return to sin. Their shameful behavior can only be compared to dogs eating their vomit and washed pigs wallowing in the mud:

> If, after they have escaped the defilements of the world through the knowledge of our Lord and Savior Jesus Christ, they are again entangled in them and overpowered, the last state has become worse for them than the first. For it would have been better for them never to have known the way of righteousness than, after knowing it, to turn back from the holy commandment that was passed on to them. It has happened to them according to the true proverb, "The dog turns back to its own vomit," and, "The sow is washed only to wallow in the mud." (2 Pet 2:20–22)

Perhaps no ancient document has expressed with more clarity the idea that the first followers of Jesus had on justification than the Shepherd of Hermas: "I have heard from some teachers, Lord—I said—that there is no repentance apart from the one that came when we descended into the water and received forgiveness for the sins formerly committed. He said to me: 'You have heard well, for that is so. For the one who has received forgiveness of sins must sin no more, but live in holiness'" (Herm. 31).

This is exactly what Paul said. This passage is even more remarkable because the author of the Shepherd finds himself in a difficult situation. On one hand he permits one exception to the general rule; on the other hand he wants to reaffirm the validity of the general rule. He announces that the apostates of the recent persecution may return to the grace of God. "The one who has sinned and repented must be taken back. . . . But not repeatedly; for there is only one repentance for God's servants" (Herm. 29). The exceptional possibility offered to the apostates, however, should not persuade the faithful members of the church to forget their responsibilities and to take their salvation for granted. Paradoxically, being baptized put the believers in Christ in a harsher position than the heathen, who still have the opportunity to take advantage of the gift of forgiveness "until the last day": "If sin still occurs, now that this day has been set a limit, they will not find salvation, for repentance for the righteous [i.e., the baptized followers of Jesus] is at an end; the days of repentance for all the saints are over, although for the heathen [i.e., those who have never been baptized] there is the possibility of repentance until the last day. . . . If you continue to add to your sins, you will receive from the Lord the opposite. All these things the shepherd, the angel of repentance, commanded me to write" (Herm. 6, 25).

When the eschatological connection between justification by faith and the imminence of the last judgment faded in the life experience of the Jesus believers, Christian theology had a hard time explaining the relationship between forgiveness of sins and salvation "according to each one's deeds." New sets of questions arose: Should the infant be baptized, or should baptism be postponed for as long as possible? May baptism be repeated, and if so, how many times? Are all sins "mortal" for the baptized, or otherwise what separates them from the grace they have received?[23] Once the apocalyptic urgency ceased, it seemed reasonable to many "to postpone repentance and baptism, a postponement based on the desire to enjoy one's life for the meantime and to get the utmost benefit for the forgiveness granted in baptism," as was the case with Constantine or Junius Bassus.[24] The delay of the end, not Augustine or Luther, is primarily responsible for the misunderstanding of the original apocalyptic message of Paul the Jew.

Conclusion

Christian theology has taken *justification* as a synonym for *salvation*. But this is not the case. In Paul's understanding, justification is "forgiveness, cleansing, and purification of past sins" and "an emancipation from sin as

23. Everett Ferguson, *Baptism in the Early Church: History, Theology, and Liturgy in the First Five Centuries* (Grand Rapids: Eerdmans, 2009).

24. Joachim Jeremias, *Infant Baptism in the First Four Centuries* (London: SCM Press, 1960), 88.

a ruler over humankind,"[25] based on "faith in Christ." Salvation is instead the outcome of the final judgment according to each one's deeds.

Equating justification by faith (which Paul preached to sinners) with (eternal) salvation by faith (which Paul never preached) is one of the major distortions of the Christian reinterpretation of Paul. It transformed the apocalyptic lament over the power of evil into an ontological impossibility of doing good, as if the sin of Adam made it impossible to live a righteous life. And it transformed the eschatological gift of forgiveness offered by God to "the many" (i.e. sinners) into the necessary prerequisite for salvation for each and every individual.

Westerholm finds it "inconceivable that [Paul] meant to distinguish an anticipatory justification based on faith . . . from a final justification based on a different criterion (performance of 'works of the law')."[26] This is, however, what the Book of Parables did, and what the Synoptics did, and what all the documents of the earliest Jesus movement, and, in the most explicit terms, what 1 Clement does. The idea of justification by faith (only for repentant sinners) and God's last judgment according to each one's deeds (for everybody) coexist harmoniously in Second Temple Jewish apocalyptic texts as well as in early Christian texts. There is an absolute continuity between Jewish apocalyptic sources and early Christian sources. There is no reason to assume that Paul thought otherwise. Unlike the Lutheran Paul, the New Perspective Paul, or the two-path Paul, the apocalyptic Paul is perfectly at home within Second Temple Judaism as well as within the early Jesus movement.

Paul saw no difference between Jewish and gentile sinners or between the lost sheep of the house of Israel and the lost sheep among the nations. They are both justified by the same gracious act of forgiveness. It is this equality element of his theology that more than any other made Paul the apostle to the gentiles and caused some controversy even within the Jesus movement.

25. VanLandingham, *Judgment & Justification*, 245.

26. Westerholm, *Justification Reconsidered*, 84.

Chapter 8

Paul the Apostle to the Lost Sheep among the Nations

A Controversial Figure

We can understand why Paul was viewed with suspicion by other Second Temple Jews (especially his former Pharisaic companions), who did not share the apocalyptic idea of the superhuman origin of evil and rejected his emphasis on the mission of forgiveness accomplished by Jesus the messiah. But Paul was also a controversial figure within the early Jesus movement. Why? His teaching, centered on forgiveness of sins, was not radically different from that of the other apostles, yet Paul's letters betray a continuous climate of controversy. The answer cannot be attributed only to a natural suspicion toward a person who had long been regarded as an "enemy" and, by his own admission, persecuted the church.

It has been traditional in modern Pauline scholarship (starting from Ferdinand Christian Baur and the Tübingen School of Theology) to attribute the controversy between Paul and other members of the Jesus movement to the struggle between the Jewish and Christian factions within early Christianity. It had to be this way; the Hegelian framework required that the new thesis (Paul's Christianity) defeat its antithesis (Peter, James, and their attachment to Judaism) in order to make room for the superior synthesis of Christianity with the Gospel of John. Consequently, Paul was praised as the one who opposed Jewish particularism in the name of a universalistic understanding of religion and emancipated Christianity from Judaism. But this approach, as we have seen, is totally anachronistic and overtly ideological.

Paul called himself the "apostle to the Gentiles" (Rom 11:13) and in Galatians 2:8 the phrase appears to be used as a distinctive identity marker in relation to Peter, "an apostle to the circumcised." There were indeed elements in Paul's theology that differentiated him from other leaders of the Jesus movement (like Peter and James). While some seemed more interested in the restoration of the twelve tribes of Israel (as attested, for instance, in the incipit of the Letter of James), in Paul there is a special emphasis on the inclusion of gentiles.

But what did Paul really mean by claiming to be the apostle to the gentiles? Reading Paul as a Second Temple Jew is a call to avoid easy simplifications and a reminder that the actual situation was far more complex and diversified than what might appear at first sight.

Competing Models of Inclusion of Gentiles: God-Fearers and Proselytes

Paul the apostle to the gentiles was not the first Second Temple Jew to preach to gentiles and to promote the inclusion of gentiles in the religion of Israel. Long before Paul, Hellenistic Jews had already developed models of inclusion of gentiles into their communities as "God-fearers."[1]

Many non-Jews found Judaism attractive as a monotheistic religion and because of its moral teachings. "The mass have long since shown a keen desire to adopt our religious observances; and there is not one city, Greek or barbarian, nor a single nation, to which our custom of abstaining from work on the seventh day has not spread. . . . As God permeates the universe, so the law has found its way among all humankind" (Josephus, *Ag. Ap.* 2.282–284). They were not proselytes but sympathizers whose moral goal was to live according to the natural law. Josephus says in generic terms that Moses "gives them a gracious welcome, holding that it is not family ties alone which constitute relationship but agreement in the principle of conduct" (*Ag. Ap.* 2.210).

1. Terence L. Donaldson, *Judaism and the Gentiles: Jewish Patterns of Universalism to 135 CE* (Waco, TX: Baylor University Press, 2008).

For Philo righteous gentiles can be more formally united to the Jews, since Judaism is not the religion of the Jewish people only, but also of the entire cosmos. "We ought to look upon the universal world as the highest and truest temple of God" (*Spec.* 1.66). The Jews are by birth the priests of humankind. "A priest has the same relation to a city that the nation of the Jews has to the entire inhabited world" (*Spec.* 2.163). This is why the Jewish high priest wears a robe which is "a copy and representation of the world." It is a reminder for him not only to live according to the natural law but also that his service is "on behalf of the whole human race" (*Spec.* 1.97). "For God intends that the high priest should in the first place have a visible representation of the universe about him, in order that from the continual sight of it he may be reminded to make his own life worthy of the nature of the universe, and secondly, in order that the whole world may co-operate with him in the performance of his sacred rites" (*Spec.* 1.96). As the sons of Levi are by birth the priests in Israel, so Jews are by birth the priests of humankind. United in the common quest for justice, gentile God-fearers have a recognized role as the laypeople in the universal religion.

Not everybody agreed. The episode of King Izates of Adiabene shows that there was a heated debate within Second Temple Judaism about the right way to include gentiles. "A certain Jewish merchant, whose name was Ananias" (Josephus, *Ant.* 20.34) instructed the king to be a God-fearer. Ananias told him "that he might worship God without being circumcised, even though he did resolve to follow the Jewish law entirely; which worship of God was of superior nature to circumcision" (*Ant.* 20.41). But then "a certain other Jew came out of Galilee, whose name was Eleazar, and who was esteemed very skillful in the learning of his country" (*Ant.* 20.43). Having found the king "reading the law of Moses," he rebuked him for not being circumcised, and invited him to put into practice what is written in the law: "O King, you are unjustly breaking the principal of those laws, and are injurious to God himself, for you should not only read them, but chiefly practice what they enjoin you" (*Ant.* 20.44). The king concluded that he should no longer delay circumcision: "He retired to another room, sent for a surgeon, and did what he was commanded to do" (*Ant.* 20.46).

The different teachings of Ananias and Eleazar about conversion are expressed with a language that echoes the controversy between the Letter of Aristeas and the Prologue of Sirach about what is more important—whether hearing or reading, the significance or the letter. "The good life consists in observing the law, and this aim is achieved by hearing much more than by reading," says the Letter of Aristeas (Let. Aris. 127). The Greek translation of the Torah has the same dignity as the Hebrew text, since it delivers the same meaning. The Prologue of Sirach instead insisted on the superiority of the reading: "You are invited therefore to read it with goodwill and attention, and to be indulgent in cases where, despite our diligent labor in translating, we may seem to have rendered some phrases imperfectly. For what was originally expressed in Hebrew does not have exactly the same sense when translated into another language. Not only this book, but even the law itself, the prophecies, and the rest of the books differ not a little when read in the original" (Sir Prologue 15–26).

The Jesus Movement and Gentiles

It was not Paul the apostle to the gentiles who began the debate within the early Jesus movement on the inclusion of gentiles. At first the members of the new messianic group did not seem very interested in reaching out to gentiles. The problem of forgiveness was not presented as if it were an exclusive or even primary problem of gentiles. The sinners whom John the Baptist and Jesus called to repentance were Jews, not gentiles.

The gift of eschatological forgiveness was intended as a special gift reserved exclusively or primarily for the sinners among the children of Israel: "Go nowhere among the Gentiles, and enter no town of the Samaritans, but go rather to the lost sheep of the house of Israel" (Matt 10:5–6). The inclusion of a few gentiles was tolerated as an exception to the rule without denying that the gift was offered to the "children," as in the story of Jesus meeting with the Syrophoenician woman: "[Jesus] said to her, 'Let the children be fed first, for it is not fair to take the children's food and throw it to the dogs.' But she answered him, 'Sir, even the dogs under the table eat the children's crumbs'" (Mark 7:27–28; Matt 15:21–28). Matthew in particular finds the faith of the woman truly admirable ("Woman, great is your faith!," Matt 15:28), but not before repeating that this remained only an exception ("I was sent only to the lost sheep of the house of Israel," Matt 15:24). Such an explicit exclusion of the gentiles from the special gift of forgiveness did not preclude the presence of the "righteous among the nations" in the world to come, since the last judgment will take place "according to each one's deeds"; but certainly it sounded odd in an environment, like that of Luke, where a large number (if not the majority) of the baptized were now gentiles. For this reason, Luke entirely omits the narrative.

Besides the Syrophoenician woman, only one other close encounter of Jesus with a gentile is recorded in the synoptic tradition. The meeting with "a centurion" at Capernaum in Matthew (8:5–13) and Luke (7:1–10), however, seems nothing more than wishful thinking, since the parallel text in John (4:46–53) speaks of "a royal official" who in the days of Jesus under Herod Antipas would have been Jewish. Matthew and Luke inherited an updated version of the narrative to reflect the new experience of the church and to offer Jesus the opportunity to praise the faith of gentiles and foretell their salvation in the kingdom of God: "Truly I tell you, in no one in Israel have I found such faith [= Luke 7:9]. I tell you, many will come from east and west and will eat with Abraham and Isaac and Jacob in the kingdom of heaven" (Matt 8:10–11).

However, things changed rapidly. In the mid-first century, the Jesus tradition needed stories to support their experience of the now pervasive presence of gentile members, and yet Acts still portrays the early community as completely unprepared. "The goal of the earliest mission, after all, had been to bring the good news to Israel. And the positive pagan response to the movement's apocalyptic message had most likely caught the early apostles off-guard: no plan for such a contingency was in place."[2]

2. Paula Fredriksen, *Paul the Pagans' Apostle* (New Haven: Yale University Press, 2017), 94.

That Jesus himself left no instruction on the integration of the gentiles is the only thing that appears clear.[3] Also in Acts, Luke shows the early followers of Jesus delivering their message of forgiveness only to Jews. "God exalted him at his right hand as Leader and Savior that he might give repentance to Israel and forgiveness of sins" (Acts 5:31–32).

According to Acts, the first followers of Jesus neither planned any campaigns toward gentiles, nor did they initiate the baptism of gentiles. It came at the gentiles' request. The first baptism of a gentile was the work of Philip the Evangelist, a Hellenistic Jew and a companion of Stephen, not one of the first disciples of Jesus or one of the Twelve. Philip joined the movement only after the death of Jesus and even in this case he did not approach the eunuch, presented as a God-fearer well acquainted with the Scriptures of Israel, with the intention of baptizing him. The meeting was not planned, and it was the eunuch who abruptly confronted Philip with the direct question: "What is to prevent me from being baptized?" (Acts 8:36).

The story of the centurion Cornelius, also a God-fearer (Acts 10:2, 22), follows the same pattern. For the apostles who "were presumably not accustomed to the mixed demography of synagogues in the Diaspora,"[4] it must have been very hard indeed to embrace the new perspective. Only reluctantly did Peter accept Cornelius's invitation. It took a vision from heaven, repeated three times, to appease his many doubts: "What God has made clean, you must not call profane" (Acts 10:15; 11:9). The decision to baptize Cornelius and his family did not come from a positive and premeditated commitment but, again, in the form of a rhetorical question. "Can anyone withhold the water for baptizing these people who have received the Holy Spirit just as we have?" (Acts 10:47).

The news of the event, we are told, was met with great criticism at Jerusalem by circumcised members (Acts 11:1–3). The surprise was not that gentiles also would be present in the world to come; this idea was not foreign to the apocalyptic tradition and to the Jewish tradition at large. What the first followers of Jesus found surprising was that the same gift of

3. Fredriksen, *Paul the Pagans' Apostle*, 30.
4. Fredriksen, *Paul the Pagans' Apostle*, 95.

eschatological forgiveness was offered to both Jews and gentiles: "God has given even to the Gentiles the repentance that leads to life" (Acts 11:18). The author of Acts puts into Peter's mouth a speech that Paul also could have uttered: "I truly understand that God shows no partiality, but in every nation anyone who fears him and does what is right is acceptable to him. . . . Everyone who believes in him receives forgiveness of sins through his name" (Acts 10:34–35, 43).

Paul's Personal Role

In all these events Paul the apostle to the gentiles had no role. He was not the first Jesus-follower to preach to and baptize gentiles. For several years after joining the Jesus movement, he did not distinguish himself in any way for any particular initiative aimed at reaching out to gentiles. Acts says that it was Barnabas who "went to Tarsus to look for Saul, and when he had found him, he brought him to Antioch" (Acts 11:25–26). Acts 13:1 mentions Paul as the last in the list of the leaders ("prophets and teachers") of the community of Antioch, after "Barnabas, Simeon who was called Niger, Lucius of Cyrene, Manaen a member of the court of Herod the ruler."

Eventually Paul joined Barnabas on a missionary journey that is generally called "Paul's first missionary journey" but should rather be called "Barnabas's first missionary journey," as Paul (who is mentioned second after Barnabas in Acts 13:2, 7) was his helper, a subordinate role that even non-Jews perceived. On the streets of Lystra, when the two preachers were mistaken as gods, the crowds seemed to have a clear understanding of the relation between the two: "Barnabas they called Zeus, and Paul they called Hermes, because he was the chief speaker" (14:12). Paul may have had brilliant oratory skills, but the head of the missionary expedition was Barnabas, not Paul.

The Acts of the Apostles tells us that after Barnabas and Paul returned to Antioch, a dispute arose in the early church about whether gentile believers should "be circumcised and ordered to keep the law of Moses" in order to "be saved" (Acts 15:1–5). The opinion is attributed to "some believers who belonged to the sect of the Pharisees" (Acts 15:5)—a sign that the divisions within

Judaism tended to replicate within the early church, as had already happened with the coming of Hellenistic Jews (the "Hellenists" led by Stephen).

According to Paula Fredriksen, the pressure that baptized God-fearers received to be circumcised and become proselytes came from some Jesus-followers as a possible reaction to the "delay of the end": "They began to insist that Gentiles in the movement formally affiliate to Israel by receiving circumcision."[5] Whatever reason was behind this move, Barnabas and Paul opposed it and led a delegation from Antioch to Jerusalem to discuss the matter "with the apostles and the elders." Both Peter and James agreed with Barnabas and Paul that "no further burden" should be imposed on the gentile believers. They were asked to "abstain only from things polluted by idols and from fornication and from whatever has been strangled and from blood" (Acts 15:20). In other words, the leaders of the early church agreed on the solution already adopted with success by the Hellenistic-Jewish communities in their relations with the God-fearers. "This meant no idols. But it also meant no circumcision: gentiles-in-Christ were to remain gentiles, up to and through the End."[6] They were included in the new movement without becoming proselytes. Here Paul played an active role in the collective decision shared by all in the end. He does not seem to have had a personal, distinctive position yet.

According to Acts, even when Paul established himself as the apostle to the gentiles he did not dramatically change the dynamics of the early mission of the Jesus-followers. Paul continued to preach "in the synagogues with the Jews and the devout persons" (Acts 17:17), visiting the main centers of the Jewish diaspora of the time, reaching out to God-fearers who had already embraced belief in the God of Israel. When in Athens "some Epicureans and Stoic philosophers . . . brought him to the Areopagus," his attempt to announce the "unknown god" to "the Athenians and the foreigners living there" resulted in a rather awkward speech and a semi-disastrous outcome, which convinced him to leave the city for the more comfortable Jewish environment of Corinth (Acts 17:18–8:1). What was it then that made Paul the champion of the gentiles?

5. Fredriksen, *Paul the Pagans' Apostle*, 103.
6. Fredriksen, *Paul the Pagans' Apostle*, 104.

The harsh reality was that the apparent unanimity of the Council of Jerusalem had not solved all the problems, as evidenced by Paul's Letter to the Galatians. Provided that gentile believers were not required to be circumcised or to keep the law of Moses, controversy exploded on the relationship between Jews and gentiles within the community, especially during communal meals. The Jewish-Hellenistic model did not imply equality; although worshipers of the same religion, by birth Jews were priests and God-fearers were laypeople. Should they sit at separate tables or might they share the same table? The incident at Antioch would soon reveal the profound divisions on this issue between Paul on one side and Peter, James, and Barnabas on the other.

The Law and the Power of Sin

Some Jews in the first century would have resisted the notion of sitting at the same table with gentiles. "Joseph never ate with the Egyptians, for this was an abomination to him" (Jos. Asen. 7:1). Joseph even refused Aseneth's chaste kiss of welcome: "It is not fitting for a man who worships God, who . . . will eat blessed bread of life and drink a blessed cup of immortality . . . to kiss a strange woman who . . . eats from their table bread of strangulation and drink from their libation a cup of insidiousness" (Jos. Asen. 8:5–6). Cornelius was "a devout man who feared God with all his household . . . and prayed constantly to God . . . an upright and God-fearing man, who [was] well spoken of by the whole Jewish nation" (Acts 10:2, 22), yet Peter expressed to him similar concerns: "You yourselves know that it is unlawful for a Jew to associate with or to visit a Gentile" (Acts 10:28).

It is true, however, that the Letter of Aristeas reveals that at least some Hellenistic Jews under certain circumstances permitted Jews and gentiles to share the same table, as the seventy-two sages who translated the Torah into Greek did at the court of the king.[7] What was a practice

7. On the Letter of Aristeas, see Benjamin G. Wright, *The Letter of Aristeas* (Berlin: deGruyter, 2015).

of Hellenistic Judaism was not shared by everyone. Already the distinction between the Hellenists and the Hebrews and the accusation by the Hellenists of having been neglected during the communal meals seems to indicate a certain tension between the two groups within the earliest Jesus movement (Acts 6:1–6).

The "people who came from James" opposed the sharing of tables between Jews and gentiles, whereas Paul favored it. Peter was caught in the middle. At first he conformed to the practice of the church of Antioch (Hellenistic Jews had no problem sharing the same table with God-fearers) but after the delegation from James arrived, Peter "drew back." Barnabas also followed his example. We don't know if they did it out of conviction, or as an act of hospitality and respect for the guests who came from Jerusalem, or as Paul insinuates, "for fear of the circumcision faction" (Gal 2:12). What we know is that this time Paul reacted vehemently, confronting Peter "to his face" and accusing him and Barnabas of "hypocrisy" (Gal 2:11, 13).

In the Letter to the Galatians, Paul reiterates his opposition to the idea that gentile believers should be required to become proselytes and circumcise. Correctly, Mark Nanos understands that "Paul opposed non-Jews becoming Jews after they became followers of Jesus."[8]

First of all, Paul reminds his readers that this has been the practice of the church for years, not only in Antioch but also in Jerusalem: when "I went up again to Jerusalem with Barnabas . . . [to meet] the acknowledged leaders. . . . Even Titus, who was with me, was not compelled to be circumcised, though he was a Greek" (Gal 2:1–3). But being a kind of defense lawyer of the gentiles is not enough for Paul. He presents himself as "an apostle—sent neither by human commission nor from human authorities, but through Jesus Christ" (Gal 1:1), bearer of a gospel that "is not of human origin" but was given to him "through a revelation of Jesus Christ" (Gal 1:11–12). He transformed the rejection of proselytism and the practice of eating together into a theological problem, making it a question of principle, the center of his distinctive gospel, and the starting point of a distinctive theology. It is now that Paul the Jesus-follower discovered

8. Mark Nanos, *Reading Paul within Judaism* (Eugene, OR: Cascade Books, 2017), 131.

himself as the apostle to the gentiles, "set . . . apart [by God] before I was born and called . . . through his grace . . . so that I might proclaim [Christ] among the gentiles" (Gal 1:15–16). For Paul, baptized gentiles should not be treated in the new movement as a separate group of God-fearers but as equal members of the community.

It is in this context that Paul first talked of justification by faith in Christ as opposed to justification by the works of the law: "We ourselves are Jews by birth and not Gentile sinners; yet we know that a person is justified not by the works of the law but through faith in Jesus Christ. And we have come to believe in Christ Jesus, so that we might be justified by faith in Christ, and not by doing the works of the law, because no one will be justified by the works of the law" (Gal 2:15–16). The gift of forgiveness that Jewish and gentile sinners have received in Christ is completely independent of the Mosaic torah, since the law has no power over cosmic evil and no power to justify sinners.

Once again, the problem is not the law, but the power of sin. Justification annuls the punishment of the law: "Christ redeemed us from the curse of the law by becoming a curse for us" (Gal 3:13). But for Paul there is no contradiction between the law of Moses and the promise of justification to sinners apart from the law, which God "made to Abraham and his offspring . . . Christ" (Gal 3:16). The law, which was given to Moses 130 years after the promise of justification to the sinners, "does not annul a covenant previously ratified by God, so as to nullify the promise" (Gal 3:17). On the other hand, "Is the law [that grants salvation to those who obey it, but does not provide justification] opposed to the promises of God? Certainly not!" (Gal 3:21). The law "was added because of transgressions, until the offspring [Jesus] would come to whom the promise had been made" (Gal 3:19). The law was "our disciplinarian until Christ came, so that we might be justified by faith" (Gal 3:24). Now that the gift of justification has been revealed in Christ, those who have been baptized "belong to Christ. . . . You are Abraham's offspring, heirs according to the promise" (Gal 3:29).

Hence, not only do gentiles not need to become proselytes in order to be saved, but by becoming proselytes they would demonstrate that the justification they received in Christ is somehow related to the law, which it is not. "Listen! I, Paul, am telling you that if you let yourselves be circumcised, Christ will be of no benefit to you. . . . For in Christ Jesus neither circumcision nor uncircumcision counts for anything; the only thing that counts is faith working through love" (Gal 5:1–6). If the law had power over cosmic evil, the sacrifice of the Christ would be pointless: "I do not nullify the grace of God; for if righteousness comes through the law, then Christ died for nothing" (Gal 2:21).

Slaves of Sin, Equal in Sin

At the Council of Jerusalem, all the followers of Jesus apparently agreed on this point: gentile sinners were justified by the same eschatological gift given to Jewish sinners ("in cleansing their hearts by faith [God] has made no distinction before them and us," Acts 15:9). But the incident at Antioch was not a rematch of the Council of Jerusalem. Paul's hard stance led him to formulate a distinctive theology. Whereas Hellenistic Judaism united Jews and gentile God-fearers in a common quest for righteousness, Paul exploited the pessimistic apocalyptic view of the sinfulness of human nature to affirm the "equality in sin" of Jews and gentiles who had joined the new movement. He argued that for both Jews and gentiles the gift of forgiveness of sins by the Christ came into effect "by faith only." The gift was completely gracious since no prerequisites could be placed on humans, who in this world are "slaves" under the power of sin. For Paul this is what the law itself teaches in the "allegory" of Hagar and Sarah (Gal 4:21–5:1). The children of Hagar are those who obey the law living "in slavery" under the power of sin, and the children of Sarah are those who have been freed from this evil world through the promise of justification: "For freedom Christ has set us free. Stand firm, therefore, and do not submit again to a yoke of slavery" (Gal 5:1).

The slavery that Paul mentions in Galatians and in Romans is not slavery to the law; it is slavery to the cosmic evil powers controlling the universe, the "elemental spirits" of Galatians 4:3, "beings that by nature are not gods" (4:8). In the Enochic tradition, people (Jews and gentiles alike) are struggling against the influence of evil forces and the temptation of the devil. Paul radicalizes this view and envisions a postwar scenario where "all, both Jews and Greeks, are under the power of sin" (Rom 3:9). Adam and Eve lost the battle against the devil and, as a result, all their descendants were "enslaved to sin" (Rom 6:6).

Slavery was a consolidated social institution in the Roman Empire. When Paul was talking of people defeated and enslaved as a result of war, he was "speaking in human terms" (Rom 6:19) that everyone could understand.[9] Everyone knew exactly what the implications of slavery were for the slaves and their children. Once the fight was over, slaves were expected to resign themselves to their condition until they died. Josephus voices the common sense of his time when he addresses the inhabitants of besieged Jerusalem and reminds them that "Fighting for liberty is a right thing, but ought to have been done at first. . . . To pretend now to shake off the yoke [of the Romans] was the work of such as had a mind to die miserably, not of such as were lovers of liberty. . . . It is a strong and fixed law, even among brute beasts, as well as among men, to yield to those that are too strong for them" (*J.W.* 5.365–67). The Romans admired and honored those who bravely fought for liberty but despised rebellious slaves and condemned them to the cross. No one could expect the devil to be weaker than the Romans.

Does this mean that all slaves are evil? Not necessarily. Once again, this was a matter of common experience. Being a slave (even the slave of an evil master) does not necessarily equate to being a sinner. However, a slave (especially the slave of an evil master) is in a very difficult situation since the slave is not free, and at any time, the master could command the slave to do evil things—a precarious and terrifying situation for anyone who wants to be righteous: "With my mind I am a slave to the law of God, but with my flesh I am a slave to the law of sin" (Rom 7:25).

The slave's only hope is for somebody to pay the redemption price and set the slave free. Such is for Paul the blood of Jesus, "effective through faith" (Rom 3:25). A conscious yes is the only thing that can be required of

9. John Byron, *Slavery Metaphors in Early Judaism and Pauline Christianity: A Traditio-Historical and Exegetical Examination* (Tübingen: Mohr Siebeck, 2003).

a slave, as nothing else could be required of someone who has no freedom. This is the situation of all sinners according to Paul. Jews and gentiles are equal in sin; the gift of forgiveness by the Christ comes into effect by faith only.

Hence, there can be no distinction between Jewish and gentile members, because they were equally sinners and were equally justified by the grace of God through Jesus Christ. As for justification—"the righteousness that comes from faith"—Jews cannot claim any superiority, unless the grace of God is denied. "For there is no distinction, since all have sinned and fall short of the glory of God; they are now justified by his grace as a gift, through the redemption that is in Christ Jesus, whom God put forward as a sacrifice of atonement by his blood, effective through faith" (Rom 3:22–25). The paradox is that gentiles show much more enthusiasm than Jews in taking advantage of the gift of justification. For Paul this is the cause of "great sorrow and unceasing anguish in my heart" (Rom 9:2). "Gentiles who did not strive for righteousness, have attained it, that is, righteousness through faith; but Israel, who did strive for the righteousness that is based on the law, did not succeed in fulfilling that law" (Rom 9:31).

In Paul's view righteousness by faith does not annul or replace but complements righteousness by works, since the last judgment will be for everybody according to each one's deeds. "We will all stand before the judgment seat of God. . . . So then, each of us will be accountable to God" (Rom 14:10–12). The problem with part of Israel is that that they do not accept the apocalyptic teaching of the Jesus-followers that in the imminence of the last judgment God in Christ has now offered another possibility of righteousness apart from the law, based on faith and not on works. The Jews have "a zeal for God, but it is not enlightened" (Rom 10:2), and they do not understand what in Paul's view was announced by the law itself. "Now, apart from law, the righteousness of God has been disclosed, and is attested by the law and the prophets, the righteousness of God through faith in Jesus Christ for all who believe" (Rom 3:21–22). In this sense, "Christ is the end of the law so that there may be righteousness for everyone who believes" (Rom 10:4). The eschatological gift is offered to both Jews and gentiles alike with "no distinction. . . . The same Lord is Lord of all and is generous to all who call on him" (Rom 10:12).

Those Jews who have accepted this offer might be "a remnant" (Rom 11:5), but the presence of some of them among the believers, including Paul himself, proves that "God has not rejected his people" (Rom 11:1–2). The Jews are and remain the holy people of God: "They are Israelites, and to them belong the adoption, the glory, the covenants, the giving of the law, the worship, and the promises; to them belong the patriarchs, and from them, according to the flesh, comes the Messiah" (Rom 9:4–5).

The "hardening" of part of Israel had a providential result as "salvation has come to the Gentiles" (Rom 11:11); "their rejection is the reconciliation of the world" (11:15). This situation, although regrettable, is only temporary: "a hardening has come upon part of Israel, until the full number of the Gentiles has come in. And so all Israel will be saved" (11:25–26). Gentile believers do not have to boast. They were grafted as "a wild olive shoot . . . to share the rich root of the olive tree" (11:17). They should therefore always "remember that it is not you that support the root, but the root that supports you" (11:18).

Opposition to Paul

The idea that the "blood of Christ" is the ransom paid for forgiveness of sins was widespread in the early Jesus movement. We find it in the most explicit terms in the Gospel of Matthew ("the Son of Man came . . . to give his life as a ransom for many," Matt 20:28), as well as in 1 Peter ("[It was] not with perishable things like silver or gold [that you were redeemed] but with the precious blood of Christ," 1 Pet 1:18–19) and Revelation ("by your blood you ransomed for God saints from every tribe and language and people and nation," Rev 5:9).

Paul and the Pauline tradition after him insisted on the complete graciousness of the event: "[We] were bought with a price" (1 Cor 6:20; 7:23). "In him we have redemption through his blood, the forgiveness of our trespasses, according to the riches of his grace" (Eph 1:7). "By grace you have been saved, through faith, and this is not your own doing; it is the gift of God—not the result of works" (Eph 2:8–9). Not everybody, however, agreed with this view. Martin Luther correctly saw in the Letter of James the major critic of Paul, but dismissed it as "a straw letter" expressing the traditional view of "Judaism."[10] This is not the case. On the only occasion when James speaks about the law, he does so in the same terms as Paul: "Whoever keeps the whole law but fails in one point has become accountable for all of it. For the one who said, 'You shall not commit adultery,' also said, 'You shall not murder.' Now if you do not commit adultery but if you murder, you have become a transgressor of the law" (Jas 2:10–11).

This is exactly what Paul says in the Letter to the Galatians, based on Deuteronomy 27:26: "All who rely on works of the law are under a curse; for it is written, 'Cursed is everyone who does not observe and obey all the things written in the book of the law.' . . . Once again I testify to every man who lets himself be circumcised that he is obliged to obey the entire law" (Gal 3:10; 5:3). For James, as for Paul, the problem is not the law but the superhuman power of evil, which makes it difficult for humans to obey the law. For many, facing God's judgment means being destined for an inevitable condemnation. Therefore, another path must be offered to sinners, a path of justification based on God's mercy. Both Paul and James saw in Jesus the agent of a gift of grace and forgiveness apart from the law.

For Paul, as we have seen, "Christ redeemed us from the curse of the law" (Gal 3:13). For James hope lies in the certainty that at the last judgment God's mercy will triumph over God's justice for those who have repented and followed the "law of liberty" preached by Jesus: "So speak and so act as those who are to be judged under the law of liberty. For judgment is without mercy to anyone who has shown no mercy; mercy triumphs over judgment" (Jas 2:12–13).

There is, however, a profound difference between the two leaders of the early Jesus movement, but this difference is not what divided Christianity from Judaism, nor even the Jesus-followers from the Pharisees. It is a

10. Preface to the so-called *Septemberbibel* of 1522

problem that derives from a different emphasis on the superhuman power of evil. James firmly rejected the Pauline idea that humans are "slaves of sin."

James's language is very similar to what we find in the Christian Testaments of the Twelve Patriarchs.[11] There we read that the devil has a key to direct access to the human self—that is, the "seven spirits of deceit" placed by Beliar within and against humankind (cf. T. Reu. 2:1–2). These spirits are human desires; once a person "is subjected to the passion of desire and is enslaved by it" (T. Jos. 7:8), losing integrity, that person is led to the "deadly sin" (*hamartia eis thanaton*; T. Iss. 7:1).

The "double tongue" is at the same time the symbol and the most evident manifestation of the internal struggle that affects all humans. God wants all his creatures to love "in simplicity of heart" (T. Iss. 7:7), while Beliar "knows no simplicity" (T. Ben. 6:7). For James as well, "the tongue is a fire. The tongue is placed among our members as a world of iniquity; it stains the whole body, sets on fire the cycle of nature, and is itself set on fire by hell. . . . No human being can tame the tongue—a restless evil, full of deadly poison. . . . From the same mouth come blessing and cursing. My brothers and sisters, this ought not to be so" (Jas 3:2–12).

James agrees with the Testaments of the Twelve Patriarchs that the source of evil is the world of iniquity—that is, the devil, whose power is manifested in the apparently uncontrollable emergence of passions: "Those conflicts and disputes among you, where do they come from? Do they not come from your cravings that are at war within you? You want something and do not have it; so you commit murder. And you covet something and cannot obtain it; so you engage in disputes and conflicts" (Jas 4:1–2).

Consequently, the Pauline series of causes and effects is significantly modified. For Paul sin is the origin of all passions ("sin . . . produced in

11. The Testaments of the Twelve Patriarchs is in the present form a Christian composition. The extent to which the document was based on pre-Christian texts is a matter of discussion among scholars. Here we refer to it as evidence of a stream of thought within the early Jesus movement, which the Testaments of the Twelve Patriarchs seems to share with the Letter of James. See Robert A. Kugler, *Testaments of the Twelve Patriarchs* (Sheffield: Sheffield Academic Press, 2001).

me all kinds of covetousness," Rom 7:8); both desire and death are consequences of the power of sin. For James, on the other hand, humans, though under temptation, are still fighting against desire, fomented by the devil, which leads to sin, which, once committed, leads to death: "No one, when tempted, should say, 'I am being tempted by God'; for God cannot be tempted by evil and he himself tempts no one. But one is tempted by one's own desire, being lured and enticed by it; then, when that desire has conceived, it gives birth to sin, and that sin, when it is fully grown, gives birth to death" (Jas 1:13–15).

Temptation is "a test" and those who successfully overcome it "will receive the crown of life that the Lord has promised to those who love him" (Jas 1:12). God, "with whom there is no variation or shadow due to change" (1:17), demands of humankind an equally simple, undivided love: "Adulterers! Do you not know that friendship with the world is enmity with God? Therefore whoever wishes to be a friend of the world becomes an enemy of God. Or do you suppose that it is for nothing that the scripture says, 'God yearns jealously for the spirit that he has made to dwell in us'?" (4:4–5).

Human beings find themselves torn between two opposite principles, enemies to themselves in their own ambivalence, and yet not slaves, since they are not entirely deprived of freedom and simplicity. Slavery is a threat and a possible outcome of the struggle, not the status of humankind. The entire spirituality of James is inspired by a positive sense of doing good. "If any think they are religious, and do not bridle their tongues but deceive their hearts, their religion is worthless. Religion that is pure and undefiled before God, the Father, is this: to care for orphans and widows in their distress, and to keep oneself unstained by the world" (Jas 1:26–27).

The gift of justification brought by Christ is also seen as a step in the ongoing struggle against the devil. It is not an unconditional gift but the result of a synergy between humans and God: "[God] gives all the more grace; therefore it says, 'God opposes the proud, but gives grace to the humble.' Submit yourselves therefore to God. Resist the devil, and he will flee from you. Draw near to God, and he will draw near to you. Cleanse your hands, you sinners, and purify your hearts, you double-minded. Lament and mourn and weep. Let your laughter be turned into mourning and your joy into dejection. Humble yourselves before the Lord, and he will exalt you" (Jas 4:6–10).

If only a yes can be asked of sinners since they are slaves of sin, there is no room for works and justification is by faith only. If, on the other hand, sin is a temptation and sinners maintain a certain degree of freedom, then they can, and should be asked to, prove their faith with some works. The Letter of James makes this move by claiming that "a person is justified by works and not by faith alone," and that "faith apart from works is barren" (Jas 2:19–26).

Not surprisingly, the Letter of James does not even mention the death of Jesus. The preaching of Jesus, the "law of liberty" Jesus taught, is the prerequisite for justification, whereas for Paul the sacrificial death of Jesus is the only thing that counts as a unilateral and gracious act of mercy.

Did Paul Abolish the Distinction between Jews and Gentiles?

The Pauline concept of justification by faith was not the divide between Christianity and Judaism but the theological rationale for affirming the equality between Jewish and non-Jewish sinners within the church. For James, being a torah-observant Jew was an advantage, because the gift of forgiveness requires some human action. Thanks to the torah, Jews have a better grasp of the devil's temptation and are better equipped to follow the law of liberty preached by Jesus. On the other hand, the Pauline metaphor of slavery leaves room only for a personal yes. It makes meaningless the idea of prerequisites or any claim of superiority of the Jews over the gentiles. Therefore, there is no basis for any claim for a distinction between the two groups within the new community. Paul's conclusion was that the gift of eschatological justification was equally offered to Jews and gentiles apart from the law and that both must exercise the same act of faith (no works whatsoever) in order to receive it. There is no distinction between Jewish and gentile sinners. Both were justified by a completely gracious act (the death of the messiah), which they accepted by faith only. There is therefore complete equality between Jews and gentiles in the way they were justified.

The same gospel was offered "to everyone who has faith, to the Jew first and also to the Greek" (Rom 1:16).

Does this mean that Paul abolished the distinction between Jews and gentiles in this world *tout court*? Paul's contemporaries were divided. There were rumors, suspicions, and accusations that Paul taught "all the Jews living among the Gentiles to forsake Moses, and [told] them not to circumcise their children or observe the customs" (Acts 21:21). Not even Paul's zeal in performing the rituals of temple purification prevented the charge at Jerusalem that he taught "everyone everywhere against our people, our law, and this place [i.e., the Temple]" (21:28). According to Acts, these were all lies since there were "many thousands of believers . . . among the Jews, and they are all zealous for the law" (21:20) and Paul was no exception—he also "observe[d] and guard[ed] the law" (21:24). Gentile believers, on the other hand, lived as God-fearers; they "abstain from what has been sacrificed to idols and from blood and from what is strangled and from fornication" (21:25).

Today's scholars are divided too. The traditional view that Paul made one people of the two by forming a new "race"[12] is openly challenged by a growing number of specialists who share the opposite view, from Pamela Eisenbaum ("The Gentile will not become Jew, and the Jew will not become Gentile")[13] to Paula Fredriksen ("Paul maintains, and nowhere erases, the distinction between Israel and the nations").[14]

Paul's autobiographical statement in 1 Corinthians 9:19–23 ("I have become all things to all people, that I might by all means save some") has been traditionally taken as evidence of his indifference to the problem. He no longer considered himself bound to the law of Moses except for reasons of opportunity "to avoid giving scandal," feeling free to observe or not observe the laws of Moses according to the circumstances.[15] It is difficult

12. Love L. Sechrest, *A Former Jew: Paul and the Dialectics of Race* (Edinburgh: T&T Clark, 2009).

13. Pamela Eisenbaum, *Paul Was Not a Christian: The Original Message of a Misunderstood Apostle* (New York: HarperOne, 2009), 255.

14. Fredriksen, *Paul the Pagans' Apostle*, 114.

15. John J. Collins, *The Invention of Judaism: Torah and Jewish Identity from Deuteronomy to Paul* (Oakland: University of California Press, 2017), 164.

to imagine, however, that Paul wanted to present such a negative portrait of himself, as someone who was engaged by his own admission in rather questionable, opportunistic behavior, thus confirming his opponents' worst suspicions.

As Nanos has shown, "becoming like signifies not behaving like, but rather arguing like."[16] Paul was not engaged in deceptive behavior; he adjusted his message to his various audiences, taking into account their different sensibilities. Paul's pastoral strategy of "rhetorical adaptability" cannot be taken as evidence that he was no longer a torah-observant Jew and preached Jewish believers in Christ to forsake the law. Paul saw no conflict between the law and the promise. Being no longer "under the law" (1 Cor 9:20) meant for him that he was no longer under the power of sin and was justified in Christ, not that he was free from the obligations of the Mosaic covenant.

Significantly, Paul's famous saying about the equality between Jews and gentiles comes in a broader context that included "male and female" and "slave and free." These are the categories that in this world represent the basic divisions of ethnos, gender, and social status: "There is no longer Jew or Greek, there is no longer slave or free, there is no longer male and female; for all of you are one in Christ Jesus" (Gal 3:28). The three groups are mentioned together, one after the other, again in 1 Corinthians 7 and, with the omission of "women," in the parallel passages of 1 Corinthians 12:13 ("we were all baptized into one body—Jews or Greeks, slaves or free—and we were all made to drink of one Spirit") and Colossians 3:11 ("There is no longer Greek and Jew, circumcised and uncircumcised, barbarian, Scythian, slave and free; but Christ is all and in all!"). Remarkably, both in the authentic letters of Paul and in the Pauline tradition, Paul's attitude toward gentiles is never presented in isolation, but always in connection with his attitude toward the other fundamental divisions of this world.

Modern interpreters have noticed that the same tensions and ambiguities affect each and every one of these categories, as attested by the history of the reception of Paul. In the nineteenth century, the Letter to

16. Nanos, *Reading Paul within Judaism*, 26–29, 98–99.

Philemon was mentioned by abolitionists and anti-abolitionists in support of their own opposite conclusions.[17] At the turn of the twentieth century *The Woman's Bible* and George Bernard Shaw condemned Paul as "the eternal enemy of woman,"[18] whereas some contemporary feminist theologians today would praise him for his liberating message about women, a message then "betrayed" by his followers.[19]

Where modern interpreters see inconsistencies and ambiguities, for the apocalyptic Paul there seems to be no ambivalence. He treated all three categories exactly the same way.

On one hand, Paul insists that "in Christ" there is perfect equality, which derives from their common condition of sin and the absolute graciousness of their justification. Such equality is particularly apparent in the communal meals in which the new community gathers before the angels (1 Cor 11:10) and already anticipates the reality of the world to come. There, Jews and non-Jews sit at the same table and eat the same food, women prophesy, and slaves are brothers.

Equality during communal meals seems to have been a constant concern in Paul's preaching. In 1 Corinthians 11:17–34 he berates the Corinthians because they turned the communal meals into a place of division and inequality. "When you come together, it is not really to eat the Lord's supper. For when the time comes to eat, each of you goes ahead with your own supper, and one goes hungry and another becomes drunk. What! Do you not have homes to eat and drink in? Or do you show contempt for the church of God and humiliate those who have nothing?" (1 Cor 11:20–22).

Even Paul's admonition to "welcome those who are weak in faith" (Rom 14:1) finds its most proper setting in the eschatological context of the communal meals. "Some believe in eating anything, while the weak eat

17. Robert Bruce Mullin, "Biblical Critics and the Battle over Slavery," *Journal of Presbyterian History* 61 (1983): 210–26; John Byron, *Recent Research on Paul and Slavery* (Sheffield: Phoenix Press, 2008).

18. Elizabeth Cady Stanton, ed., *The Woman's Bible*, vol. 2 (New York: European Pub. Co., 1898); George Bernard Shaw, "Preface on the Prospect of Christianity" (1912).

19. Kathy Ehrensperger, *That We May Be Mutually Encouraged: Feminism and the New Perspective in Pauline Studies* (London: T&T Clark, 2004); Karen Armstrong, *St. Paul: The Misunderstood Apostle* (London: Atlantic Books, 2015).

only vegetables. . . . Some judge one day to be better that another, while others judge all days to be alike" (Rom 14:2, 5). The explicit reference to the "kingdom of God" indicates that Paul is talking about an issue that does not concern this world but the world to come: "The kingdom of God is not food and drink but righteousness and peace and joy in the Holy Spirit" (14:17). Communal meals are mystical moments in which the members of the community partake with the angels and are one in Christ as they will be in the world to come. Paul is "persuaded in the Lord Jesus that nothing is unclean in itself" (14:14). Peace and harmony, however, are important and suggest prudence and tolerance toward those who are weak, even in an eschatological context in which there should be full "equality": "Those who eat must not despise those who abstain, and those who abstain must not pass judgment on those who eat. . . . Those who observe the day, observe it in honor of the Lord . . . since they give thanks to God; while those who abstain, abstain in honor of the Lord and give thanks to God" (Rom 14:3, 6).

On the other hand, it does not appear that for Paul equality is a criterion applicable to everyday life. The same Paul who allowed women to prophesy at the communal meals before the angels, having received a "symbol of authority" in Christ (1 Cor 11:10), says that "the husband is the head of his wife" (11:3) and that women should be "silent" in the public assemblies of the church as is customary in this world (14:33–36). Likewise, he reminds Philemon that he and Onesimus are now brothers but falls short of asking him to free all his slaves.

In 1 Corinthians 7 the general recommendation to "remain in the condition in which you were called" (7:20) is directed to males and females (husbands and wives, married and unmarried, 7:1–16), Jews and gentiles (circumcised and uncircumcised, 7:17–20), slaves and masters (7:21–24). From the perspective of the early Jesus movement, the coming of Christ and the rapid approaching of the eschaton ("the appointed time has grown short," 7:29) have radically modified human relations ("the present form of this world is passing away," 7:31) but not yet abolished the divisions of ethnicity, gender, and social status. Jews remain Jews, gentiles remain gentiles, and males and females and slaves and owners all remain in their present status. The (first) coming of the Christ has made possible the establishment of nonconflicting relations. In the words of Nanos, "it is fundamental to the truth of the Gospel that difference remains, that social boundaries are acknowledged, but that discrimination should not."[20]

What Karin B. Neutel has defined as the "cosmopolitan ideal" of Paul[21] was neither a philanthropic nor philosophical move nor the political manifesto of a social reformer but the result of the apocalyptic tension between this world and the new reality of the world to come. The kingdom of God is not yet established on earth but has already been inaugurated by the coming of the messiah.

Consistently, the Pauline tradition would proclaim the end of the "hostility" between Jews and gentiles in this world ("[Jesus] is our peace; in his flesh he has made both groups into one and has broken down the dividing wall, that is, the hostility between us," Eph 2:14) in the same way that males and females, slaves and masters, are now invited to live their relationships in love and harmony: "Wives, be subject to your husbands. . . . Husbands, love your wives" (Eph 5:22–33; Col 3:18–19); "Slaves, obey your earthly masters. . . . Masters, treat your slaves justly and fairly" (Eph 6:5–9; Col 3:22–4:1).

Speaking of slaves and masters and men and women who joined the Jesus movement, Lucy Peppiatt also reached similar conclusions: "They now ate together in a church setting. . . . So although in the society of the time becoming a Christian didn't lead directly to a change in status, when they were worshipping together in church, their social status was overridden by their status 'in Christ.' . . . They were all one. You could say that the church was supposed to be a little taste of heaven."[22]

This is precisely how things are in Paul's apocalyptic perspective regarding Jews and gentiles. Equality "in Christ" is an eschatological status, not yet a completely fulfilled reality in this world. Except when they gather

20. Nanos, *Reading Paul within Judaism*, 40.

21. Karin B. Neutel, *A Cosmopolitan Ideal: Paul's Declaration 'Neither Jew Nor Greek, Neither Slave Nor Free, Nor Male and Female' in the Context of First-Century Thought* (London: Bloomsbury T&T Clark, 2016).

22. Lucy Peppiatt, *Unveiling Paul's Women: Making Sense of 1 Corinthians 11:2–16* (Eugene, OR: Cascade Books, 2018), 19.

for communal meals, Paul expected the circumcised members of the community to be torah-observant and the gentile members to live as God-fearers. He expected Jews and gentiles to behave precisely as husbands and wives and masters and slaves. Made mystically equal "in Christ" (but not yet equal in this world), they should live in this world in harmony and mutual love (but not in equality), according to their own distinct identities. Ethnic, gender, and social categories are not abolished and will not be abolished in this world. Jews and gentiles, husbands and wives, masters and slaves will continue to live as such in this world until they enter the kingdom of God, where all these distinctions will be finally abolished. Then (and only then) will that "taste of heaven" they already experience in the communal meals become their permanent status.

Conclusion

Paul was not the first Jew to preach to the gentiles and was not the first follower of Jesus to baptize a gentile. He, however, made himself the "apostle to the Gentiles" (Rom 11:13). He saw no difference between Jewish sinners and gentile sinners, or between the lost sheep of the house of Israel and the lost sheep among the nations. They were all slaves under the power of evil and justified by the same faith in Christ, who offered himself for their redemption. Christ's blood was the price of their freedom. Paul advocated equality within the new community of faith. He turned a (practical) problem of the relations between Jews and gentiles (their sitting at the same table during communal meals) into the starting point of a distinctive theology that he summarized in his concept of justification by faith only. In order to maintain the distinction between Jews and gentiles, Paul's opponents spoke, rather, of eschatological forgiveness as a gift conditioned on faith *and* works.

Paul proclaimed the equality "in Christ" of Jews and gentiles, men and women, free and slaves—the collapse of divisions of ethnos, gender, and social status. All will be kin, no one will be an enemy, yet none of these categories is or will be completely abolished in this world. Paul asks Philemon to welcome his slave Onesimus as a brother in Christ, yet does not tell Philemon to free all his slaves using the argument that in Jesus Christ there is no longer slave or free. Paul mentions Priscilla before her husband, Aquila, in the ministry of Christ (Rom 16:3–4), and yet he reiterates that "the husband is the head of his wife" (1 Cor 11:3) whereas he could have stated that in Jesus Christ there are no longer males and females. Paul proclaims the end of all enmity between Jews and gentiles in Christ, and yet why should he have claimed only in this case that such a distinction is no longer valid? If the ideals of the first Christians included, as Hans Dieter Betz argued, "the abolition of the religious and social distinctions between Jews and Greeks, slaves and freemen, men and women,"[23] nobody noticed it in antiquity, certainly not slaves and women, to whom equality was not granted even when the church had the power to do it. Ironically, Christian theology very soon stressed the absolute and definitive end of the distinction between Jews and gentiles as a divine decree in this world, here and now, but did not take an equally strong stance about the abolition of any distinction of gender and social status. Paul either abolished all three categories or did not abolish any of them.

23. Hans Dieter Betz, *Galatians: A Commentary on Paul's Letters to the Churches in Galatia*, Hermeneia (Philadelphia: Fortress, 1979), 190.

Chapter 9

Paul the Herald of God's Mercy toward Sinners

Not a Prophet of Doom

This analysis restores the image of Paul as a preacher of God's love and mercy, not as a preacher of hatred and intolerance. Paul was not a prophet of doom who condemned to hell all (Jews and gentiles alike) who do not admit to being sinners and do not believe in Jesus Christ. Paul was the herald of God's mercy toward sinners (Jews and gentiles alike).

The traditional Lutheran view of Paul highlighted the centrality of grace and correctly understood justification by faith as a gracious act of God's mercy. "Sinners for whom Christ died are declared righteous by God when they place their faith in Jesus Christ."[1] However, by transforming the apocalyptic lament over the power of evil into an ontological impossibility of doing good, Augustine and Luther turned Paul's good news of the eschatological gift of forgiveness offered by God to sinners through Jesus into the necessary prerequisite for salvation for all. Paul's message was that all human beings (Jews and gentiles alike) are "under the power of sin" (Rom 3:9), but not that they are all condemned. Although limited, human free will has not been destroyed by original sin, and the last judgment remains "according to each one's deeds" (Rom 2:6).

1. Stephen Westerholm, *Justification Reconsidered: Rethinking a Pauline Theme* (Grand Rapids: Eerdmans, 2013), 22.

E. P. Sanders's *Paul and Palestinian Judaism* (1977) was a landmark, a masterpiece.[2] It redeemed Pauline studies from the most derogatory anti-Jewish elements, in particular disproving that the opposition between grace and law was the irreconcilable divide between Christianity and Judaism. Sanders's conclusions, however, need to be revisited and updated. Paul did not present, as Sanders concluded, "an essentially different type of religiousness from any found in Palestinian Jewish literature,"[3] nor did he "explicitly deny that the Jewish covenant can be effective for salvation, thus consciously denying the basis of Judaism."[4]

The time is ripe for a new paradigm that, without refuting the achievements of the past, can incorporate the new results of research that come from contemporary studies on Second Temple Judaism and Christian origins. We no longer need to separate Paul from Judaism in order to claim his Christianness, nor do we need to separate him from the early Jesus movement in order to state his Jewishness. As a first-century Jewish religious leader, Paul did not live in isolation and in total theological uniqueness but was equally at ease in Second Temple Judaism and in the early Jesus movement (and much more closely related to the contemporary synoptic tradition and Acts than generally thought).

A Proud Jew and a Proud Follower of Jesus

Paul was a Second Temple Jew. He was born, lived, and died as a Second Temple Jew. Nothing ever changed in his primary religious and ethnic identity. Like all Second Temple Jews, Paul shared the idea that God had called all humans to righteousness, having revealed to them God's will (what is good and what is evil)—to the Jews according to the torah, to the gentiles according to the natural law embedded in each one's conscience. There is no "excuse" or "partiality": in the end the judgment will be "according to each one's deeds" (Rom 2:1–11).

2. E. P. Sanders, *Paul and Palestinian Judaism: A Comparison of Patterns of Religion* (London: SCM, 1977).

3. Sanders, *Paul and Palestinian Judaism*, 543.

4. Sanders, *Paul and Palestinian Judaism*, 551.

Raised a Pharisee, Paul became a leader of the early Jesus movement. His decision to join the Jesus movement was not conversion but a move within Judaism, from one Jewish group to another. In the diverse world of Second Temple Judaism, what changed was not his being a Jew but his way of being a Jew—his understanding of Judaism. By adhering to the new faith as a first-century Jewish follower of Jesus, he not only acquired a sense of the imminent coming of the end and the belief in Jesus as the messiah, but also changed his worldview by joining a messianic apocalyptic movement. He embraced the apocalyptic view of the superhuman origin of evil and saw sinners not only as individuals responsible for their own actions but also as victims of evil and in need of being freed from the power of sin by a gracious intervention of God that at the end of time will justify those who repent.

The good universe created by God was disrupted by the rebellion of the devil and his hosts. This cosmic rebellion, which took place apart from the law, has corrupted the world and limited the human ability to obey God's will, making it harder (though not impossible) for the individual to be righteous. Because of the fall of the disobedient son of God, Adam (seduced and defeated by the devil), all humans (Jews and gentiles alike) are affected by the power of evil—they are "under the power of sin." Paul went so far as to say that Satan's victory over God's disobedient son, Adam, caused all humans (Jews and gentiles alike) to become "slaves of sin."

In the garden of Eden, the devil won the day but not the war against God. God is omnipotent and merciful. The triumph of evil was temporary, not only because the good angels in heaven have already defeated the fallen angels, but also because God in God's mercy has now intervened to counterbalance the power of evil on earth through the mission of his obedient Son, Jesus. There is perfect symmetry between the two sons of God, Adam and Jesus; as is the power of evil, so is the power of grace. The fall of Adam caused evil to spread apart from the law and limited human freedom; so also the obedience of Jesus caused grace to spread apart from the law and restored human freedom. The fall of Adam caused many to become sinners; so also the death and self-sacrifice of Jesus the messiah caused many to become righteous—all those (Jews first and gentiles alike) who have faith in him as God's agent of justification.

Paul expected that all sinners (Jews and gentiles alike), having been justified by this gracious act and cleansed of their past sins, would fill their lives with good works and, with the help of God, would remain "blameless on the day of our Lord Jesus Christ" (1 Cor 1:8) and be reckoned among the righteous at the last judgment. Jesus, "the Son of Man [who] has authority on earth to forgive sins" (Mark 2:10; Matt 9:6; Luke 5:24), will soon return as the final judge. "The Lord himself, with a cry of command, with the archangel's call and with the sound of God's trumpet, will descend from heaven" (1 Thess 4:16) to execute the last judgment "according to each one's deeds," as the savior of the righteous (Jews and gentiles alike) and of (former) sinners who, having repented and been justified by faith, have remained righteous in Christ. Only the unrepentant will be condemned.

Unlike other members of the Jesus movement, Paul refused to accept that baptized gentiles had a different or lower status within the church. He could not see any distinction between a Jewish sinner and a gentile sinner: both were "slaves of sin" and forgiven "by faith only." This does not mean that he advocated the abolition of the distinction between Jews and gentiles in this world. On the contrary, as in the case of gender and social distinctions, he accepted it as an inevitable (perhaps even providential) reality to be mitigated but not abolished until the establishment of the world to come, where these distinctions would eventually disappear. Having received as a Jew the gift of eschatological forgiveness promised by Jesus to the lost sheep of the house of Israel, Paul decided to devote his life to the lost sheep among the nations. As the apostle to the gentiles he claimed he was called by Jesus specifically to be the messenger of this opportunity of justification to gentile sinners, whereas other apostles concentrated on Jewish sinners.

Paul believed that justification came apart from the law and was an eschatological gift to be received by faith alone, but he never intended it as an exclusive path to salvation, since the universal last judgment will be according to each one's deeds. He never questioned the validity of the torah or believed that the law was too difficult to be observed; his only concern was the difficulty that people "under the power of sin" have in obeying the law. Paul was a torah-observant Jew who believed that justification by faith was an eschatological gift offered through Jesus the messiah to all sinners (not only to the gentiles) in the imminence of the final judgment. Does this mean that he believed that Jews should abandon the obedience of the torah and that no Jew could be saved without baptism? Not at all.

While repeating the common Jewish teaching that "all people are sinners," Paul shared the apocalyptic idea that humankind is divided between the righteous and the unrighteous. But now the time of the end has come, and the possibility of receiving justification through forgiveness has been offered to the unrighteous who repent. Paul preached to the gentiles, but his message was neither addressed only to the gentiles nor pertinent solely to them. Exactly the same gospel was announced to the Jews and the gentiles—the good news of the gift of forgiveness to sinners: "I had been entrusted with the gospel for the uncircumcised, just as Peter had been entrusted with the gospel for the circumcised" (Gal 2:7). The only difference was that Peter preached God's forgiveness to the lost sheep of the house of Israel, while Paul preached the same message to the lost sheep among the nations.

Paul certainly had a pessimistic view of the power of evil. He compared the situation of humankind to a population defeated and enslaved by the devil, but he would have shared the principle that only the sick need a physician. The sick include Jews and gentiles alike, though not all of them: the righteous (Jews and gentiles alike) do not need a physician (Mark 2:17; Matt 9:12–13; Luke 5:31–32).

No One Is Excluded: Jews, Gentiles, Sinners

Once placed in their original Jewish apocalyptic context, even the most complex and difficult passages of Paul recover their coherence and clarity to acquire unexpected resonances in today's world.

The implications for Christian theology, and in particular for relations between Christians and Jews, are of paramount importance. Paul was not supersessionist; he never intended justification by faith as a substitute for judgment according to each one's deeds or a replacement of the Mosaic torah. He expected all those justified and now living in Christ to be saved because their past sins had been forgiven and their life was now full of good deeds. But he did not take it for granted, not even for himself; justification by faith was a way to restore (not annul) human responsibility and uphold (not abolish) God's covenants, including the Mosaic torah.

No less relevant are the implications for relations in general between Christians and followers of other religions and belief systems. To say that all humans must believe in Christ in order to be saved is a misrepresentation of Paul's preaching, since the last judgment for all will be according to each one's deeds. Also, to say that the Jews have the torah while the gentiles have Christ does not faithfully represent Paul's position. Christ is neither the *one* and exclusive path to salvation offered to all humankind nor the *second* path to salvation offered to the gentiles alongside the torah to the Jews. Rather, Christ is the *third* path to salvation offered specifically to sinners (Jews and gentiles alike), who "under the power of sin" failed to live according to the torah and the natural law, which God gave to Jews and gentiles, respectively, as effective paths to salvation for the righteous.

In Paul's view, Christ is God's gift not to all but to the many—the sinners. The righteous (Jews and gentiles alike) will be saved because of their good deeds. Paul is aware that the power of evil makes it difficult for all humankind to be righteous: for Jews to follow the torah and for gentiles to follow the natural law embedded in each one's conscience. He preaches the good news that, at the end of time, sinners (Jews and gentiles alike) are offered the extraordinary possibility of repenting and being justified in Christ by God's mercy apart from God's justice. Sinners (Jews and gentiles alike) are given a second chance to be reborn and have their past sins forgiven. Paul was not Lutheran. He never taught salvation by faith as the only path, but announced to sinners justification (that is, forgiveness of past sins) by faith. Paul did not preach two separate paths to salvation (one for Jews, one for gentiles) but rather three: righteous Jews have the torah, righteous gentiles have their own conscience, and sinners, the lost sheep of the house of Israel and among the nations who have fallen without hope under the power of evil, have Christ the forgiver.

BIBLIOGRAPHY

Ambrose, Kimberly. *Paul Among the Jews: Rehabilitating Paul*. Eugene, OR: Wipf and Stock, 2015.

Armstrong, Karen. *St. Paul: The Apostle We Love to Hate*. Boston: Houghton Mifflin Harcourt, 2015.

Arnold, Brian J. *Justification in the Second Century*. Minneapolis: Fortress, 2013.

Barclay, John M. G. *Paul and the Gift*. Grand Rapids: Eerdmans, 2015.

Baur, Ferdinand Christian. *Paulus der Apostel Jesu Christi: sein Leben und Wirken, seine Briefe und seine Lehre*. Stuttgart: Becher & Müller, 1845. 2nd rev. ed. Edited by Eduard Zeller. 1866–67.

Beker, J. Christiaan. *Paul's Apocalyptic Gospel: The Coming Triumph of God*. Philadelphia: Fortress, 1982.

———. *Paul the Apostle: The Triumph of God in Life and Thought*. Philadelphia: Fortress, 1980.

Bird, Michael F. *An Anomalous Jew: Paul among Jews, Greeks, and Romans*. Grand Rapids: Eerdmans, 2016.

Blackwell, Ben C., John K. Goodrich, and Jason Maston, eds. *Paul and the Apocalyptic Imagination*. Minneapolis: Fortress, 2016.

Boccaccini, Gabriele, ed. *Enoch and the Messiah Son of Man: Revisiting the Book of Parables*. Grand Rapids: Eerdmans, 2007.

———. *Middle Judaism: Jewish Thought, 300 BCE to 200 CE*. Minneapolis: Fortress, 1991.

———. *Roots of Rabbinic Judaism: An Intellectual History, from Ezekiel to Daniel*. Grand Rapids: Eerdmans, 2002.

Boccaccini, Gabriele, and Carlos A. Segovia, eds. *Paul the Jew: Rereading the Apostle as a Figure of Second Temple Judaism*. Minneapolis: Fortress, 2016.

Bock, Darrell, and James H. Charlesworth, eds. *Parables of Enoch: A Paradigm Shift*. London: Bloomsbury, 2014.

Boers, Hendrikus. *The Justification of the Gentiles: Paul's Letters to the Galatians and Romans*. Peabody, MA: Hendrickson, 1994.

Bousset, Wilhelm. *Die Religion des Judentums im neutestamentlichen Zeitalter*. Berlin: Reuther & Reichard, 1903; 2nd ed. 1906; 3rd rev. ed. *Die Religion des Judentums im späthellenistischen Zeitalter*. Edited by Hugo Gressmann. Tübingen: Mohr Siebeck, 1926.

———. *Kyrios Khristos: Geschichte des Christusglaubens von der Anfängen des Christentums bis Irenaeus*. Göttingen: Vandenhoeck & Ruprecht, 1913. ET: *Kyrios Christos: A History of the Belief in Christ from the Beginnings of Christianity to Irenaeus*. Translated by John E. Steely. Nashville: Abingdon, 1970.

Boyarin, Daniel. *The Jewish Gospels: The Story of the Jewish Christ*. New York: New Press, 2012.

———. *A Radical Jew: Paul and the Politics of Identity*. Berkeley: University of California Press, 1994.

Byrne, Brendan. *Paul and the Christian Woman*. Homebush, NSW: St. Paul Publications, 1988.

Campbell, Douglas A. *The Deliverance of God: An Apocalyptic Rereading of Justification in Paul*. Grand Rapids: Eerdmans, 2009.

Capes, David B. *The Divine Christ: Paul, the Lord Jesus, and the Scriptures of Israel*. Grand Rapids: Baker Academic, 2018.

Charles, Robert Henry. *Religious Development between the Old and The New Testaments*. London: Williams & Norgate, 1914.

Chialà, Sabino. *Libro delle Parabole di Enoc: testo e commento*. Brescia: Paideia Editrice, 1997.

Collins, John J. *The Apocalyptic Imagination: An Introduction to Jewish Apocalyptic Literature*. 2nd ed. Grand Rapids: Eerdmans, 1998. 3rd ed. 2016.

———. *The Apocalyptic Imagination: An Introduction to the Jewish Matrix of Christianity*. New York: Crossroad, 1984. 2nd ed.

———. *The Invention of Judaism: Torah and Jewish Identity from Deuteronomy to Paul*. Oakland: University of California Press, 2017.

Davies, J. P. *Paul among the Apocalypses?: An Evaluation of the 'Apocalyptic Paul' in the Context of Jewish and Christian Apocalyptic Literature*. London: Bloomsbury T&T Clark, 2016.

Davies, William D. *Paul and Rabbinic Judaism: Some Rabbinic Elements in Pauline Theology*. London: SPCK, 1948.

Dunn, James D. G. *The New Perspective on Paul*. Grand Rapids: Eerdmans, 2007.

———. *The Theology of Paul the Apostle*. Grand Rapids: Eerdmans, 1998.

Ehrensperger, Kathy. *That We May Be Mutually Encouraged: Feminism and the New Perspective in Pauline Studies*. London: T&T Clark, 2004.

Ehrman, Bart D. *How Jesus Became God: The Exaltation of a Jewish Preacher from Galilee*. New York: HarperOne, 2014.

Eisenbaum, Pamela Michelle. *Paul Was Not a Christian: The Original Message of a Misunderstood Apostle*. San Francisco: HarperOne, 2009.

Everling, Otto. *Die paulinische Angelologie und Dämonologie: ein biblisch-theologischer Versuch*. Göttingen: Vandenhoeck & Ruprecht, 1888.

Fee, Gordon D. *Pauline Christology: An Exegetical-Theological Study*. Peabody, MA: Hendrickson, 2007.

Flusser, David. "The Dead Sea Sect and Pre-Pauline Christianity." In *Aspects of the Dead Sea Scrolls*, edited by Chaim Rabin and Yigael Yadin, 215–66. Jerusalem: Hebrew University Press, 1958.

Fredriksen, Paula. *Paul the Pagans' Apostle*. New Haven: Yale University Press, 2017.

Gager, John J. *Reinventing Paul.* Oxford: Oxford University Press, 2000.

———. *Who Made Early Christianity?: The Jewish Lives of the Apostle Paul.* New York: Columbia University Press, 2015.

Gaston, Lloyd. *Paul and the Torah.* Vancouver: University of British Columbia Press, 1987.

Gathercole, Simon J. *Where Is Boasting?: Early Jewish Soteriology and Paul's Response in Romans 1–5.* Grand Rapids: Eerdmans, 2002.

Hägerland, Tobias. *Jesus and the Forgiveness of Sins: An Aspect of His Prophetic Mission.* Cambridge: Cambridge University Press, 2012.

Hall, Sidney G. *Christian Anti-Semitism and Paul's Theology.* Minneapolis: Fortress, 1993.

Hurtado, Larry W. *Lord Jesus Christ: Devotion to Jesus in Earliest Christianity.* Grand Rapids: Eerdmans, 2003.

Jewett, Robert. *Romans: A Commentary.* Minneapolis: Fortress, 2007.

Kabisch, Richard. *Die Eschatologie des Paulus in ihrer Zusammenhangen mit dem Gesamthegriff des Paulus.* Göttingen: Vandenhoeck & Ruprecht, 1893.

Kinzer, Mark. *Post-Missionary Messianic Judaism: Redefining Christian Engagement with the Jewish People.* Grand Rapids: Brazos Press, 2005.

Klausner, Joseph. *From Jesus to Paul.* London: Allen & Unwin, 1942.

Langton, Daniel R. *The Apostle Paul in the Jewish Imagination.* Cambridge: Cambridge University Press, 2010.

Lapide, Pinchas, and Peter Stuhlmacher, *Paulus: Rabbi und Apostel.* Stuttgart: Calwer, 1981. ET: *Paul: Rabbi and Apostle.* Translated by Lawrence W. Denef. Minneapolis: Augsburg, 1984.

Larsson, Stefan. "Just an Ordinary Jew: A Case Why Paul Should Be Studied within Jewish Studies." *Nordisk Judaistik / Scandinavian Jewish Studies* 29.2 (2018): 3–16.

Levine, Amy-Jill, ed. *A Feminist Companion to Paul.* London: T&T Clark, 2004.

Maccoby, Hyam. *The Mythmaker: Paul and the Invention of Christianity.* New York: Harper & Row, 1986.

Matlock, R. Barry. *Unveiling the Apocalyptic Paul: Paul's Interpreters and the Rhetoric of Criticism.* Sheffield: Sheffield Academic, 1996.

Montefiore, Claude G. *Judaism and St. Paul: Two Essays.* London: Max Goschen, 1914.

Moore, George F. "Christian Writers on Judaism." *HTR* 14 (1921): 197–254.

———. *Judaism in the First Centuries of the Christian Era: The Age of the Tannaim.* 3 vols. Cambridge: Harvard University Press, 1927–30.

Munck, Johannes. *Paulus und die Heilsgeschichte.* Aarhus: Universitetsforlaget, 1954. ET: *Paul and the Salvation of Mankind.* Translated by Frank Clarke. London: SCM, 1959.

Murphy-O'Connor, Jerome, ed. *Paul and Qumran: Studies in New Testament Exegesis.* London: Chapman, 1968.

Nanos, Mark D. *The Irony of Galatians: Paul's Letter in First-Century Context.* Minneapolis: Fortress, 2002.

———. *The Mystery of Romans.* Minneapolis: Fortress, 1996.

———. *Reading Paul within Judaism.* Eugene, OR: Cascade, 2017.

Nanos, Mark D., and Magnus Zetterholm, eds. *Paul within Judaism: Restoring the First-Century Context to the Apostles.* Minneapolis: Fortress, 2015.

Neusner, Jacob, William Scott Green, and Ernest Frerichs, eds. *Judaisms and their Messiahs at the Turn of the Christian Era.* Cambridge: Cambridge University Press, 1987.

Neutel, Karin B. *A Cosmopolitan Ideal: Paul's Declaration 'Neither Jew Nor Greek, Neither*

Slave Nor Free, Nor Male and Female' in the Context of First-Century Thought. London: Bloomsbury T&T Clark, 2016.

Nickelsburg, George W. E. *1 Enoch 1*. Minneapolis: Fortress, 2001.

Nickelsburg, George W. E., and James C. VanderKam. *1 Enoch 2*. Minneapolis: Fortress, 2012.

Oliver, Isaac W., and Gabriele Boccaccini, eds. *The Early Reception of Paul the Second Temple Jew*. London: Bloomsbury T&T Clark, 2018.

Parkes, James. *Jesus, Paul, and the Jews*. London: SCM Press, 1936.

Patterson, Stephen J. *The Forgotten Creed: Christianity's Original Struggle against Bigotry, Slavery, and Sexism*. Oxford: Oxford University Press, 2018.

Penna, Romano. *L'apostolo Paolo: Studi di esegesi e teologia*. Milan: Paoline, 1991. ET: *Paul the Apostle: A Theological and Exegetical Study*. Translated by Thomas P. Wahl. Collegeville, MN: Liturgical Press, 1996.

Peppiatt, Lucy. *Unveiling Paul's Women: Making Sense of 1 Corinthians 11:2–16*. Eugene, OR: Cascade, 2018.

———. *Women and Worship at Corinth: Paul's Rhetorical Arguments in 1 Corinthians*. Cambridge: James Clarke, 2017.

Pesce, Mauro. *Le due fasi della predicazione di Paolo*. Bologna: Dehoniane, 1994.

Protho, James B. *Both Judge and Justifier: Biblical Legal Language and the Act of Justifying in Paul*. Tübingen: Mohr Siebeck, 2018.

Räisänen, Heikki. *Paul and the Law*. Tübingen: Mohr Siebeck, 1983.

Roetzel, Calvin J. *Paul: A Jew on the Margins*. Louisville: Westminster John Knox, 2003.

Rudolph, David. *A Jew to the Jews: Jewish Contours of Pauline Flexibility in 1 Corinthians 9:19–23*. Tübingen: Mohr Siebeck, 2011.

Sacchi, Paolo. *L'apocalittica giudaica e la sua storia*. Brescia: Paideia, 1990. ET: *Jewish Apocalyptic and Its History*. Translated by William J. Short. Sheffield: Sheffield Academic, 1997.

———. *Storia del Secondo Tempio*. Turin: Marietti, 1994. ET: *The History of the Second Temple Period*. Translated by Thomas Kirk. Sheffield: Sheffield Academic, 2000.

Sanders, E. P. *Paul, the Law, and the Jewish People*. Philadelphia: Fortress, 1983.

———. *Paul and Palestinian Judaism: A Comparison of Patterns of Religion*. London: SCM, 1977.

Sandmel, Samuel. *The Genius of Paul*. New York: Farrar, Straus & Cudahy, 1958.

Schweitzer, Albert. *Die Mystik des Apostels Paulus*. Tübingen: Mohr Siebeck, 1930. ET: *The Mysticism of Paul the Apostle*. Translated by William Montgomery. London: Adam and Charles Black, 1931.

———. *Geschichte der Paulinischen Forschung*. Tübingen: Mohr Siebeck, 1911. ET: *Paul and His Interpreters: A Critical History*. Translated by William Montgomery. London: Adam and Charles Black, 1912.

Segal, Alan F. *Paul the Convert: The Apostolate and Apostasy of Saul the Pharisee*. New Haven: Yale University Press, 1990.

———. *Rebecca's Children: Judaism and Christianity in the Roman World*. Cambridge: Harvard University Press, 1986.

Sprinkle, Preston M. *Paul & Judaism Revisited: A Study of Divine and Human Agency in Salvation*. Downers Grove, IL: InterVarsity Press, 2013.

Stendahl, Krister. *Paul among the Jews and Gentiles*. Minneapolis: Fortress, 1976.

———. "Paul and the Introspective Conscience of the West." *Harvard Theological Review* 56 (1963): 199–215.

Stowers, Stanley K. *A Rereading of Romans: Justice, Jews, and Gentiles*. New Haven: Yale University Press, 1994.

Stuckenbruck, Loren T., and Gabriele Boccaccini, eds. *Enoch and the Synoptic Gospels: Reminiscences, Allusions, Intertextuality*. Atlanta: SBL Press, 2016.

Thackeray, Henry St. John. *The Relation of St. Paul to Contemporary Jewish Thought*. London: Macmillan, 1900.

Thiessen, Matthew. *Paul and the Gentile Problem*. Oxford: Oxford University Press, 2016.

Thomas, Matthew J. *Paul's 'Works of the Law' in the Perspective of Second Century Reception*. Tübingen: Mohr Siebeck, 2018.

Thompson, Michael B. *The New Perspective on Paul*. Cambridge: Grove Books, 1976.

Tilling, Chris. *Paul's Divine Christology*. Tübingen: Mohr Siebeck, 2012.

VanLandingham, Chris. *Judgment & Justification in Early Judaism and the Apostle Paul*. Peabody, MA: Hendrickson, 2006.

Waddell, James A. *The Messiah: A Comparative Study of the Enochic Son of Man and the Pauline Kyrios*. London: T&T Clark, 2011.

Watson, Francis. *Paul and the Hermeneutics of Faith*. London: T&T Clark, 2004.

———. *Paul, Judaism, and the Gentiles: A Sociological Approach*. Cambridge: Cambridge University Press, 1986.

Weber, Ferdinand Wilhelm. *System der altsynagogalen palästinischen Theologie aus Targum, Midrasch und Talmud*. Leipzig: Dörffling & Franke, 1880. 2nd rev. ed. *Jüdische Theologie auf Grund des Talmud und verwandter Schriften*. Edited by Franz Julius Delitzsch and Georg Schnedermann. 1897.

Westerholm, Stephen. *Justification Reconsidered: Rethinking a Pauline Theme*. Grand Rapids: Eerdmans, 2013.

———. *Perspectives Old and New on Paul: The "Lutheran" Paul and His Critics*. Grand Rapids: Eerdmans, 2004.

Witherington, Ben. *The Paul Quest: The Renewed Search for the Jew of Tarsus*. Downers Grove, IL: InterVarsity Press, 1998.

Wrede, William. *Paulus*. Halle: Gebauer-Schwetschke, 1904. 2nd ed. Tübingen: Mohr Siebeck, 1907. ET: *Paul*. Translated by Edward Lummis. London: Philip Green, 1907.

Wright, N. T. *Paul: A Biography*. New Haven: Yale University Press, 2017.

———. *Paul and His Recent Interpreters: Some Contemporary Debates*. Minneapolis: Fortress, 2015.

———. *Paul and the Faithfulness of God*. Minneapolis: Fortress, 2013.

———. *The Paul Debate: Critical Questions for Understanding the Apostle*. Waco, TX: Baylor University Press, 2015.

———. *What St. Paul Really Said: Was Paul of Tarsus the Real Founder of Christianity?* Grand Rapids: Eerdmans, 1997.

Yinger, Kent L., *The New Perspective on Paul: An Introduction*. Eugene, OR: Cascade, 2011.

———. *Paul, Judaism, and Judgment According to Deeds*. Cambridge: Cambridge University Press, 1999.

Young, Brad H. *Paul the Jewish Theologian: A Pharisee among Christians, Jews, and Gentiles*. Peabody, MA: Hendrickson, 1998.

Zetterholm, Magnus. *Approaches to Paul: A Student's Guide to Recent Scholarship*. Minneapolis: Fortress, 2009.

INDEX OF MODERN AUTHORS

SUBJECT INDEX

INDEX OF ANCIENT SOURCES